Meditation

Meditation

How to harness the power
of inner reflection

Tara Ward

ARCTURUS

In memory of my sister-in-law, Barbara Sullivan,
a sweet soul who is loved and missed by many.

All images courtesy of Shutterstock.

ARCTURUS

This edition published in 2021 by Arcturus Publishing Limited
26/27 Bickels Yard, 151–153 Bermondsey Street,
London SE1 3HA

ISBN: 978-1-3988-1317-5
AD010178US

Printed in China

Contents

What is Meditation?

Why have you picked up this book? Perhaps you know a little about meditation and like the sound of it. Perhaps you often feel that life must be something more than working, eating and sleeping.

Through meditation you can learn to enjoy every single moment of the life you have, to acknowledge and appreciate everything that is working well for you, and to turn negative scenarios into positive, encouraging ones.

Meditation has been described as "deep reflection." By becoming calm and silent and slowly withdrawing our senses from the world, we can reflect on anything and everything in a much more profound way. The deeper the reflection, the more likely we are to learn from it. The secret lies in how well we can learn to withdraw.

Meditation is a wonderful opportunity to work on your ability to focus and concentrate. It is possible to shut out distractions and irritations by learning to meditate.

VOYAGE OF DISCOVERY

One of the many joys of meditation is that it is utterly personal to you and no one else can totally share your experience. What is doubly wonderful about meditation is that it is absolutely free and can be practiced entirely in your own time!

Meditation is also more than this. It's about going quietly within to find out more about yourself and others on a deeper level. This then opens up a wealth of benefits.

It means we can learn to accept ourselves exactly as we are. It means we can understand why we are where we are in life and what we can do to shift areas of our life that appear "stuck." The simple exercises coming up will show you the way forward.

Embrace silence

Are you someone who finds silence unnerving? We have become so used to constant noise that shutting it out altogether can be unsettling. Do you always have the radio or some music on, either at home, at work or when you travel? Are you used to the sounds of people talking constantly, of traffic outside your windows, or of a neighbor's barking dog? Start to notice what sounds are around you constantly.

How often do you enjoy the natural sounds of nature? Are you aware of birdsong? Can you hear the wind rustling in the trees or the whooshing of a fast-flowing stream or river? Are there any natural sounds that you can enjoy on a regular basis near your home or workplace? If not, think about taking a trip to a park or a beach, and enjoying the peace it brings.

SWITCH OFF

Try switching off the radio, television or stereo. Let yourself experience the silence. How does it make you feel? Sometimes we actually want distracting sounds around us because we don't want to be quiet. We are afraid to sit still because we fear we might end up thinking about issues we've been trying to push into the background.

In other words, we often use sounds as a means of covering up how we are really feeling. If you know that you do this, don't worry. Meditation will gently and gradually reveal to you that you needn't be afraid of any of those emotions and worries. It can teach you to let go and release the anxieties blocking your way forward. If you are someone who relishes silence and loves the feeling of peace that it brings, then you are well on your way to enjoying meditation!

Focus on awareness

The early stages of meditation involve appreciation of what is around us. Try this simple exercise involving an item of food to work on your senses.

Choose a simple food that you are happy to eat. It can be something as simple as a single grape or a sugar cube. Hold it in your hand and look at it.

Where has it come from? Do you know anything about the manufacture of this item? Think about all the components that went into this item in your hand. Nature must have played a part somewhere, if it was grown. Rain and sun were important at one stage.

What about the people who either picked this item or put it together or worked the machines that manufactured it? How did you get it to where you are now?

Consider the item in your hand. It actually has had quite a journey to make it to you. Now, say a silent "thank you" to everyone who participated in this journey from raw ingredients to finished product. Acknowledge that everything around you has gone through a similar journey. How does that make you think and feel?

SAVOR THE MOMENT

Now eat the item, slowly, with awareness and appreciation. Notice how you feel while eating it. Is it different from how you would have felt if you had simply popped it into your mouth without stopping to think about it?

If it was a natural item, did you feel more drawn to eat it? If it was a processed item, did you feel less inclined to want to consume it? Appreciation of everything is a far more powerful and all-encompassing act than you might first suppose. This exercise is an example of meditation as an everyday, vibrant part of living.

Part One
And Breathe...

"Our minds can accomplish extraordinary tasks that often defy logical thought."

Learning to breathe

You might find this title odd. Surely you already know how to breathe! It's something you've been doing quite successfully on your own since you were born, usually unconsciously.

Yet how much do you know about your own breathing? The majority of the time, we simply breathe in and out unconsciously and constantly, without ever stopping to think about it. Do you know what is physically happening to your body every time you breathe in and out? Do you have any idea of the beauty and complexity of your breathing system?

It is through awareness of our breathing that we access every meditative state. Every human breathes every minute of every day, on average about 15 times per minute. However, how often are you aware of your breathing? How often do you notice each breath coming in and going out? The answer is probably almost never! So meditating is about awareness of the breath. Just as we discussed in the previous chapter about meditating being awareness and appreciation of everything, so awareness of your own breathing is the key to learning how to meditate.

Most of us also don't breathe deeply and fully. Meditation is about learning how to breathe deeply into the lungs, enjoying every single in and out movement, rejoicing in the power and beauty of our own breathing system. This close observation of our own breath allows us to slip effortlessly into a deeper state of relaxation and thereby enjoy a true meditative state. The process really is as basic as that. However, learning how to truly observe your breath and to focus solely on that is not quite as easy as it first sounds.

How do we breathe?

The reason we don't tend to breathe properly is the result of an underused muscle just below our lungs called the diaphragm. Every time we breathe in, the diaphragm flattens out, to allow the lungs to fill up with air. When we breathe out again, the diaphragm assumes the shape of an inverted U, helping squeeze the last of the air out of our lungs. This process is repeated every time we breathe in and out.

ARE YOU DOING IT RIGHT?

Most of us don't use our diaphragm properly. We tend to go around doing what is called shallow breathing. This means that we fill the top part of our lungs with air, but not the bottom two thirds; thus, as the diaphragm is resting on the bottom of the lungs, it is never used fully. Certain professions are exceptions to this. Opera singers and professional athletes have to learn to breathe deeply. Musicians who play wind instruments also belong in this category, as do stage actors. Anyone can learn how to breathe deeply; it simply takes a little practice.

How do you know if you are breathing deeply or not? Below is a simple exercise to check what is happening with you.

Stand in front of a mirror that shows you the top half of your body, down to your waist. Take a deep breath in and notice if your shoulders lift as you do so. Can you see them rising? If you can, then you are doing what is called shallow breathing. You are filling the top half of your lungs but not the remainder. Don't worry if this is the case for you.

Testing your diaphragm

Stand in front of your mirror. Place your hands over the lower part of your ribcage so that your middle fingers are just touching. Now take a good, deep breath in. Let your ribcage slowly and comfortably expand.

Have your fingertips moved apart just a little? If they have, you are learning to breathe deeply. If they haven't, breathe out and then take a breath in again, but this time watch your shoulders and upper chest. Are they rising again? If so, remember that you are breathing only into the top of your lungs and not further down.

Focus on your lower ribcage again. Don't force your breath; simply imagine all the air coming in and going down into the lower part of your lungs. Let your ribcage expand outward. Are your fingertips moving just a little bit apart now?

Strengthening your diaphragm

Sometimes just focusing on your fingertips can feel discouraging, as no matter how hard you focus, the ribcage doesn't seem to want to expand any distance. There are various techniques you can use to help deepen your breathing. Several exercises are detailed below, and you might want to practice these on a regular basis for a number of weeks. But remember, if you start to feel dizzy, stop. Resume your normal breathing and don't return to the exercise for at least fifteen minutes.

These exercises basically use a thought process to allow you to breathe fully without any effort. Our mind or imagination can accomplish extraordinary tasks that often defy logical thought. You probably notice this when you're daydreaming. Some people can simply close their eyes and effortlessly transport themselves somewhere else, even smelling the scents and being aware of a different atmosphere.

Stomach breathing

Many people find the following exercise quite liberating. It breaks with the conventional way of teaching breathing, and by concentrating on something you know isn't true, it becomes an enjoyable game rather than a difficult task.

Sit down in a comfortable upright chair, close your eyes and focus on your breathing. Don't try to do anything with the breath, just observe it coming in and going out. You will notice that some breaths are naturally shorter than others, some seem longer. Don't try to force your breathing into any regular pattern. Just enjoy observing it.

TRY THIS

✳ Now we're going to play a game. Next time you breathe in, imagine that your lungs are actually down in your stomach. You know they aren't, and that they rest under your ribcage, but, just for fun, let's pretend they are under your navel. Enjoy the sensation of the breath going all the way down into your stomach. Remember not to force it, just let the warm air float all the way down to your stomach area. Follow the path of the breath back up again, from your stomach, all the way up and out through your nose again. Notice how much warmer the out breath is after the inside of your body has warmed it. Keep repeating this process for a few minutes.

✳ Remember, you are not trying to breathe deeply during this, you are simply redirecting your breath to another area of your body. Don't force anything. Let the air come and go naturally and easily, but keep focusing on the thought that your lungs are in your stomach.

✳ After a few minutes, take the focus away from your stomach and let your breathing return to normal.

Balloon breathing

This exercise is another useful way of playing with your breathing and not trying to force yourself to breathe more deeply. The moment we focus on something in an intense, uncomfortable way, we create all sorts of blocks to breathing deeply and fully.

TRY THIS

✳ Sit in a comfortable upright chair and close your eyes. Start to focus on your breathing, but do not direct it in any way. Let your breath come and go naturally without forcing it. Enjoy the freedom of observing your breath without trying to control it.

✳ Now imagine that your lungs have ten little balloons inside them, five in each lung. They are tough balloons with thick skins that won't burst. The next time you breathe in, notice how many of the balloons are being blown up. Are they all inflating? If they are, increase the number of balloons in each lung. If only a few of the balloons have been half-inflated, then reduce the number to whatever feels manageable. You do not want to make this exercise hard work; it should be enjoyable.

✳ Now you want to help blow up all your balloons. Take a deep comfortable breath in and notice how the balloons fill up easily and effortlessly. Breathe out and watch them deflate again. Does it feel like they are all working properly? Keep focusing on the balloons in your lungs and keep expanding your breath, easily and effortlessly, until you feel all the balloons inflating and deflating comfortably with each in and out breath.

✳ Then let the image of the balloons fade. Return to your normal breathing. After a few minutes, open your eyes and focus on an item in the room. Make sure you have returned fully to normal breathing before you stand up.

Ribcage breathing

Once you start to discover the joys of breathing deeply, it becomes a pleasure to let yourself slip into that relaxed state, and it becomes something you can do easily and effortlessly. This is another simple exercise to improve breathing deeply into your lungs.

TRY THIS

* Sit in a comfortable upright chair and close your eyes. Start off by watching your breath as it goes in and out. Don't force it in any way, just let it come and go naturally. Sometimes it's shallow, sometimes the breath seems longer and deeper. Let it be and simply observe how it feels. Take your time.

* Now you want to think about your ribcage. Notice on the next breath in how the ribcage slowly expands outwards. Notice as you breathe out how the ribcage contracts back into the body again. Keep observing this movement of the ribcage without trying to alter it in any way.

✳ Next, you want to imagine that every time your ribcage expands, it is actually reaching further and further outwards. Keep your eyes closed as you do this. You know your ribcage isn't really extending out into the room, but play with your imagination and feel as though it is. Gradually have it expand, without trying to make it happen. Know that your thoughts are simply having fun. There is no effort involved. Even have your ribcage touch the walls of the room you are in! Imagine your ribcage as soft and free-flowing. See it billowing out around the room, effortlessly expanding and contracting. Notice how it seems to have a life of its own, easy and unrestricted. Play with this new freedom for a while.

✳ When you are ready, return to your normal breathing, and as you do so let the image of your expanding ribcage fade. If you have really lost yourself in this game and want to come back to reality, simply place your hands on either side of your ribcage. Recognize how solid and real your ribcage is now. Open your eyes and gaze at an object in the room. Wait a few minutes before standing up.

Alternate nostril breathing

Based on yogic techniques, alternate nostril breathing is a simple but incredibly powerful technique that helps to calm, ground and focus your thoughts. You won't appreciate how well this works until you experience it for yourself.

TRY THIS

✳ Close your eyes. Place your right hand over your face so that your thumb can close off your right nostril and your little finger and the finger next to it can comfortably close the left nostril. Your index and middle fingers can rest lightly against your forehead.

✳ Now you are going to close off your right nostril and breathe in through your left nostril. Close your left nostril and breathe out through your right nostril. Still keeping your left nostril closed, breathe in again through your right nostril. Close off your right nostril. Breathe out through your left nostril. Still keeping your right nostril closed, breathe in again through your left nostril and then repeat the process. After a little while you will find it is easy to get into a comfortable rhythm.

✳ As you follow the pattern, count to two slowly as you breathe in and then again as you breathe out. Gradually increase this to four as you breathe in and four as you breathe out. Once you can breathe in and out comfortably to the slow count of four, you can introduce a pause between each in and out breath. Count to two slowly in these pauses.

IN SUMMARY

Breathe in through left nostril to the count of four

Hold for two

Breathe out through right nostril to the count of four

Hold for two

Breathe in through right nostril to the count of four

Hold for two

Breathe out through left nostril to the count of four

Hold for two

Part Two
Mini Meditations

"The only thing that is
absolutely definite and real
is this actual moment."

What are mini meditations?

Now that you've had a good introduction to breathing and what it really entails, we're going to start looking at how you can incorporate short meditations into every aspect of your daily life, and the benefits it can bring you.

Mini meditations are quite quick and don't involve a lot of deep concentration. The amazing results they offer can give you just the boost you need to encourage you into the deeper realms of more prolonged meditations.

As with all the exercises in this book, taking a moment to breathe freely and deeply is important every single time you prepare for a meditation, whether it is for a very brief mini meditation or a meditation lasting for an hour or more. Your breathing is always the key to the door of possibility.

FINDING PURPOSE IN DAILY TASKS

A good way to describe these quick techniques would be as a moment of appreciation and awareness. They can encompass anything, from an item of food (as, for example, the food-appreciation exercise we did in the first chapter) to an inanimate object, an animal, or a person. A mini meditation can relate to an action you are taking, even something as simple as walking down the street. It can be done as you wash the dishes, do some shopping or sit at your desk at work. A mini meditation is a short period of time that you use to reflect on something. That something does not have to be deeply profound. You can find purpose, meaning, and good use in everything in daily life, if you want to.

Waking-up meditation

Let's start with something many people find a chore: getting up in the morning. Do you find this difficult? If motivating yourself to get up is hard work, take a few minutes after waking to work through the following:

Lie still in bed for a moment. Resist the urge to close yourself off to everything and take a few deep breaths. Tell yourself you will not sleep. Instead of focusing on what you don't like about getting up, what can you find to appreciate about this moment?

TRY THIS

Here are a few suggestions (not all of them may apply to you, but consider those that do):

✳ You have spent the night in a comfortable bed

✳ You have had a rejuvenating sleep

✳ You live in a prosperous country, free from war

✳ You have a job to go to

※ You have friends and family who love you

※ You have your health

※ Something wonderful may happen to you today

※ You have water to wash in and food to eat

※ You have clothes to put on your body

※ You are alive

Choose just one statement relevant to you and let your thoughts focus on it. Remember to keep breathing deeply and easily. What happens when you focus on one of these aspects of your life? Do you find yourself floating back into the negative with "Ah, yes, but..."? Pull your thoughts back and focus on what you can appreciate now.

When you are ready, give silent thanks for what you have and then get out of bed, resolving to allow yourself brief moments of awareness when you will appreciate what is in your life right now.

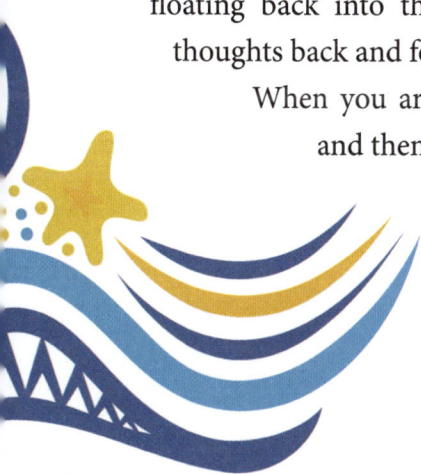

Good health meditation

Think about when you have been ill, say with a bad case of the flu. Can you remember how bad you felt, and the incredible relief when you started to feel better and your memory of the illness faded? That time when you realized you were feeling better was wonderful, wasn't it? Can you remember the enormous relief and sense of appreciation you felt when you knew you were improving? Try to recall that sensation of overwhelming gratitude and pleasure. For that moment, could you not tangibly experience how all of you felt alive, grateful and content?

However, once you recovered, did you have any lingering sense of appreciation for your good health? Did you go around daily feeling good about the fact that you were healthy and full of energy? Perhaps you did for a day, maybe half a day. Then your life no doubt returned to its usual routine and you forgot to appreciate your current state of health. That is, until you felt sick again and the cycle started to repeat itself!

What would our lives be like if we spent all our time living in a state of appreciation for what we had, constantly remembering all the positive qualities around and in us? What if every day we focused on what was good, and took the time to appreciate everyone and everything around us? For example, how do you think you would feel if you spent the majority of your time acknowledging your good health, and were aware of the pleasure and peace stemming from it?

Smiling meditation

Did you know that smiling relaxes about a hundred muscles in your face? Many of us hold so much tension there throughout the day—a smile will release that tension. Also, there is now proof that breaking into a smile actually sets off certain chemical reactions in our body that tell our brain we are happy. In other words, the simple process of smiling can make us feel better.

Think of a difficult or stressful situation. Let yourself feel the emotion for a moment. Notice that you won't want to smile! Give yourself a moment or two to worry and feel gloomy about what's happening. Look around the room you're in and notice things. Are they depressing, negative things you pick up on? Really allow yourself to feel the stress. Notice how it affects your body, your breathing, your mental and emotional state. Now choose to let it go. Let the worrying issue recede. Feel it fade into the distance. Take a moment to accomplish this. Notice if you find it hard to let go.

FEEL JOY

Now, think of something that makes you happy, something that makes you feel really good. Smile. Let it become a big, generous smile. How does it make you feel? Notice the changes you feel inside: physically, emotionally and mentally. Allow yourself to feel happy and appreciative of what you have. Look around you, wherever you are right now. How does everything seem? Can you suddenly see something nice that you hadn't appreciated before? Let yourself rest in that state for a moment. Keep smiling. You may feel the wellbeing increase and swell inside and around you. Enjoy the moment. When you're ready, stop smiling, but retain that feeling of comfort and happiness you discovered inside.

Being in the now

Most of us have trouble with the concept of enjoying each moment as it exists. We tend to live more with our thoughts in the future, or sometimes in the past, if we feel either state is preferable to the present. We want to learn how to live "in the now" and enjoy it.

A lot of people don't really understand the concept of enjoying every moment as it comes along, because they are naturally so geared up to believing life is about planning for the future and thinking ahead. Perhaps it has to do with having another child, or a bigger house, or planning for retirement. Everything becomes about the future.

But the future doesn't exist. It hasn't happened yet. You have no guarantees about what will happen to you. You also can't change anything in your past. The only thing that is absolutely definite and real is this actual moment.

FINDING VALUE

What positive changes might we be able to make if we clearly see everything around us now and take full advantage of it to shape our future? So, if we can obtain greater awareness and understand better how to find our intended path in life through being "in the now," how can we achieve that state? We can do it by constantly undertaking mini meditations that remind us who and what we are and how valuable everything we do is, no matter how slight or trivial it may seem.

Consider the routines you carry out on a daily basis, and see how you can give them more meaning and purpose. What other things do you do that you would classify as a chore, without any joy attached to them? Most people would agree that housecleaning, laundry and shopping are boring. So how can we transform them?

Shopping meditation

S tart your awareness about shopping by carefully considering what you put on your shopping list. Do you really need all the items you're writing down? How much of the food is actually healthy, and will fill you with energy and nurture your body?

Now consider where you want to shop. What stores would you like to support? Whose ethics do you value? You want to walk into the store with a smile on your face, happy to do business with the people involved.

Do you want to avoid genetically modified food? Do you prefer organic produce? Do you care that the food you eat is ethically produced, without forced labor or unfair regulations? Which countries would you like to support by buying their produce? What ingredients are harmful in the detergents we use today? What can you do about this?

These are all searching questions, and you may feel daunted by some of them. Remember, it doesn't happen all at once. Make small changes.

Notice, when you do your shopping, how different you feel. Realize that you can acknowledge and bless the people involved in the chain of actions that brings you the products you buy, from those who oversaw the creation of the raw ingredients to the person who sold you the final product.

As you walk around different stores and acknowledge the wealth of produce available to you, remember others who have so little, or virtually nothing. Take the time to send them a prayer of love and support. Awareness of others is the starting point of compassion. Without initial awareness, we will not act.

Turn the simple act of shopping into a completely aware "meditation" of seeing what is happening here and now, and using it to reassess how you want to live your life.

Waste-awareness meditation

There is nothing in life that can't be transformed into a positive action or emotion, if your attitude is that you are seeking true awareness of a situation. As an ultimate test, how about being aware of emptying your own trash? Try this exercise next time you take out the garbage.

For one week, before you throw anything into your trash can, think about what you are planning to put into it. How much of what you throw away could be recycled?

Have you ever thought about starting a compost pile with your vegetable and fruit scraps?

Do you need to use all the plastic products you have at present? Can you refill certain bottles or cut down on items that aren't strictly necessary?

SAVING THE PLANET

With every item you prepare to throw away, be aware of any use it might be put to. Can an empty jam jar become a container for something? Is that houseplant really dead, or could you take a cutting and have it regrow into a strong new plant?

When you have assessed that everything in your trash can really needs to be there, notice how much smaller the amount has become as a result of your awareness.

Notice how the awareness of what is waste and what isn't makes you rethink your lifestyle, how you eat and how you live. Besides helping you reassess your own needs, it is enabling you to shift your perception of the whole planet.

If you know that you are creating minimal waste, you know that you are doing your bit to help the planet and reduce our increasing pollution problem. One of the benefits of acting with awareness is that it affords you a greater sense of inner peace through acting responsibly and carefully.

Part Three
Going Deeper

"Meditation is often described as being about the discovery of an inner peace and stillness."

Preparing for meditation

While mini meditations don't require any preparation besides taking the time to focus on awareness and breathing, when we work at a deeper level it's important to follow guidelines that are there to nurture and protect you.

So what are we going to be doing next, and why do we have to prepare ourselves for it in a certain way? Meditation is often described as being about the discovery of an inner peace and stillness. With mini meditations, this sense is not as pronounced. You were working much more on an external level of appreciation and awareness. To go within, and discover a profound stillness and peace, requires another level of concentration and prolonged focus. You need to ease yourself into this new experience by giving consideration to a number of external aids that will help you.

Take a look at the following list. This should be your checklist for all future meditations. It's important that you follow each of the actions, especially in the early stages of learning to meditate. In the chapter ahead, you can work through each point and find out why it's necessary. Awareness of what each action entails will allow you to accept each condition and to enjoy working with it, rather than fighting it.

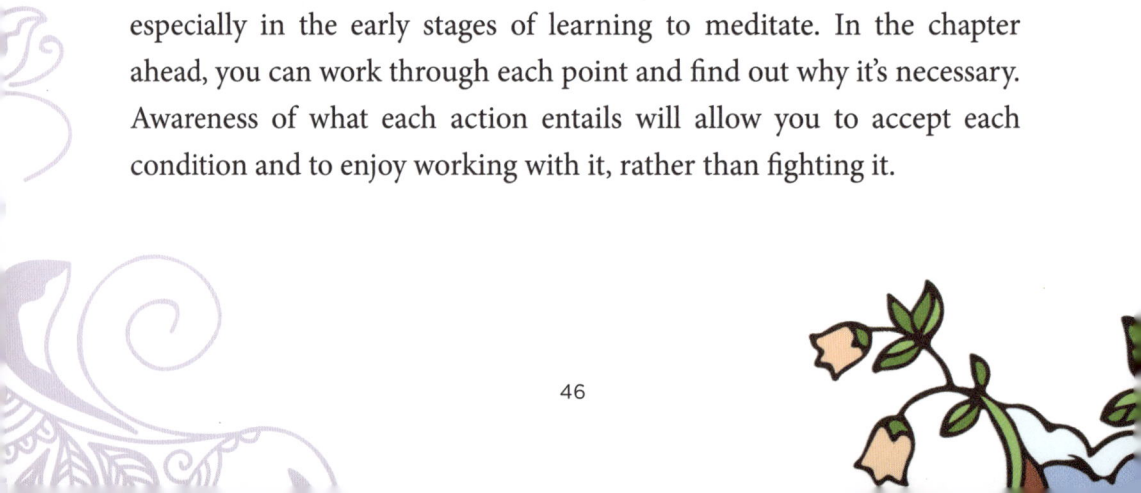

YOUR CHECKLIST

○ A quiet, undisturbed location

○ Wear loose, comfortable clothing

○ Be alcohol- and drug-free

○ A comfortable position in which
you can sit/lie completely still

○ Cleanse before you start meditating

○ Remember to breathe!

○ Place a glass of water within easy reach

A quiet, undisturbed location

This is essential. To access the wonderful world of inner awareness requires a degree of concentration. You can't concentrate if you are constantly being interrupted. You must have a quiet space where no one can disturb you. If you can't trust someone not to come in, such as an animal or a young child, then make sure you can lock the door. Put on the answering machine, switch off your cell phone, make sure everything is geared toward you not being interrupted. Make sure other people in the vicinity know that you don't want to be disturbed.

Another reason for a finding a quiet space is that some meditations leave you feeling emotional afterwards; this might take the form of a "high" or euphoria, or you might find yourself feeling quiet and subdued, needing to mull over the insights you received during meditation. Whatever your state, you may feel vulnerable for a while and want to be alone to rebalance yourself before facing the external world again. These sensations are normal and common.

Creating a sacred space

So what makes a good meditation "room"? Not everyone has the luxury of being able to create their own private space. If you only have the option of a bedroom or study, you will already have certain decor that you will probably not want to change. It doesn't matter in the sense that you can meditate anywhere, as long as it is private and you will be undisturbed.

If you do have a choice, and there's a room you can have to yourself, then the key to a meditation room can be summed up in one word: simplicity. You want to create a space that is conducive to you slipping quietly into inner peace and awareness.

What symbolizes peace to you? Most people would say white or pale pastel colors. The plainer the room the less likely you are to be distracted by the things in it.

Perhaps you might want to add something that is spiritual for you. This might be a representative of nature, such as a vase of fresh flowers, a beautiful stone or piece of driftwood. Perhaps you prefer a painting or poster of a rainbow, a body of water or a forest.

If you are fortunate enough to have your own space to decorate (and it can be very small, just big enough for you to sit in comfortably), then give serious thought to the few items you place there. Sit in awareness in your room for a while and let your own wisdom come to you and show you what is right for this space. The simpler the better.

Wear soft, loose clothing

This may seem unimportant, but the fact is that you want to help yourself in every way possible to sit quietly and relax into your meditation. There are always things to distract you as you start to focus on your breathing, and uncomfortable clothing is an easy diversion. Anything that cuts into the neck or waist stops you from focusing on your breath. Avoid fabric that's scratchy or makes you feel claustrophobic, but also make sure you are warm enough. No one will see you when you meditate; this is your time to relax and to be exactly as you want to be.

Wear those really baggy sweatpants that are loose around the waist, put on that stained sweater that's so soft and warm. You're not going to a fashion show, you're just going to be yourself in a totally relaxed state, so you might as well make the most of it.

It's best not to wear anything on your feet while meditating. You want to be as unrestricted as possible. The feet are also useful as a means of grounding yourself when you bring yourself back to reality afterwards, and it's easier to feel grounded without footwear.

Think about colors too. Do you find certain colors more soothing than others? If you find bright red stimulating, it might not be a good choice for meditation clothing.

If you find you're drawn to particular clothing when you practice meditation, then keep them purely for that purpose. No one else needs to see you in them, and you can be comfortable and cozy in your own space.

Avoid drugs and alcohol

This is a must. Alcohol and drugs do not mix with meditation. Even one glass of wine or a strong painkiller can get your mind working in a way that is not remotely compatible with altered states of awareness. Never, ever drink or take drugs and then try to meditate.

Why is this so important? One of the experiences you may have during meditation is a sense of being protected, nurtured and guided by other energies around you. It manifests itself as a faint but lovely feeling of warmth and comfort that slowly comes over you and permeates your body. It is a great joy when it happens, and once you've experienced it, you can't wait for the next time. Alcohol and drugs distort the mind, which can have an unsettling effect and is the opposite of feeling protected and nurtured.

It is also easier not to meditate with a full stomach, as you will find yourself constantly being distracted by your rather heavy and bloated stomach. A light meal is better. Preferably, though, wait several hours after eating before you meditate.

Get comfortable

To enter a deeper meditative state, you want to try to maintain a motionless, comfortable position. This may not always be possible, but it is your goal.

Sitting in a straight-backed chair, with your hands resting comfortably on your lap with palms facing up, is a great way to meditate because your body is in natural alignment. It's best if you can keep a right angle between your upper and lower legs, and for your upper legs to be parallel to the floor. Again, this is to place as little strain on your body as possible. If you need to sit on a thicker pillow or cushion, or even put something like pile of books under your feet to make this work, then it's a good idea to do so.

If you want to experiment with lying down for meditation, lie flat on your back with your legs stretched out, a short distance apart. Your arms should rest straight out on the floor, a foot or so away from your body, with the palms facing up. Your head should be in a straight line with the rest of your body, and you should be looking up at the ceiling. This position puts the least strain on your body while allowing it to be in alignment. The main problem with lying down is that it is so tempting to go to sleep, particularly if you're tired!

If for whatever reason neither of these positions is comfortable for you, don't worry. It is the fact that you have a clear intention of learning how to meditate that is of paramount importance. Although certain positions are naturally more conducive for meditative states, you can meditate in any position as long as you are able to relax and focus on your breathing without feeling restricted in any way.

Cleansing techniques

If you want to attain stillness and go into a state of inner peace and awareness, you will find it difficult if you're constantly thinking about everyday problems. You have to learn how to let them go while you are meditating.

Try this cleansing technique to let go of the everyday worries and stresses before you meditate.

Close your eyes. Focus on your breathing for a moment, but don't force it in any way. Wait until you feel your breathing slow down and deepen before you continue.

You are going to create a cleansing sanctuary that is your own personal space. It belongs solely to you, and it will be of your own personal design. This is an opportunity for your fertile mind to create something wonderful. You may know it doesn't exist in the real world, but here in the wonderful realm of your imagination anything is possible, and you are going to enjoy the creation process.

What do you find most cleansing and comforting? It may be warm water from a bathtub or shower, or fast-flowing, cool water from a stream or river. It could be hot sunlight or soft, gentle rain. Maybe you just want to imagine pure, brilliant white light streaming down from above as a spiritual or religious cleansing. This is your chance to create what is most powerful for you. Give yourself some time to think about what is most appealing. Choose a scenario that you find both comforting and nurturing.

When you have created an image you like, strengthen your relationship with it by making it as vivid as possible. So if you like the thought of a shower or bath, see it clearly in your mind's eye. Where is it? What size? What color? Put big, fluffy towels and wonderful-smelling soap into the space. Take your time during this process. Savor it.

If you have opted for bright sunlight or gentle rain, where are you when this cleansing takes place? What are your surroundings? Make them as clear as possible. Feel as though you can smell, touch and hear your cleansing space, as well as see it.

If you like the thought of pure white light from above, where is its source? How does that make you feel? Where do you choose to be when this cleansing takes place? Make it as real as possible for yourself.

WASH AWAY NEGATIVITY

When you feel your cleansing sanctuary is vivid and really powerful as an image, slowly place yourself into it. Stand under that shower, sit in the sunlight, walk in the rain or experience the pure white light. How does it make you feel? You should feel all your worries, fears and problems ebbing or being washed away. This should be a real sensation for you, and it should be deeply comforting.

If you can't receive any tangible sensation of cleansing from it, then your cleansing sanctuary is not yet working for you. It should always give a feeling of peace and safety. You should feel calm, renewed and refreshed after time in your cleansing space. Work with this image all the time to make it even richer in imagery, even more powerful in its cleansing ability. You will use it often, so make sure it feels as wonderful as possible.

This cleansing sanctuary is your retreat from negative energy. You can use it any time before, during and after meditations. It can be used on a daily basis when you want to quickly wash away something unpleasant.

It is always there for you. Maintain it, and keep it clean and pure. Never let anyone else into your cleansing sanctuary. It is solely for you. Enjoy it.

Remember to breathe

This is the single most important item on your checklist, because you will accomplish very little if you don't focus on your breath. It is there as a constant reminder for you, because even though you may intend to remember the significance of your breathing at all times, there will be plenty of occasions when you forget about it completely.

Most people start off focusing on their breathing, and then completely forget about it. You need to return to the power of your breathing throughout the meditation process. Without an awareness of it, you will not be able to move onto a higher level of meditating or come to terms with a particular issue you may have been avoiding or misunderstanding. For many reasons, breathing is always and forever your golden key to meditation.

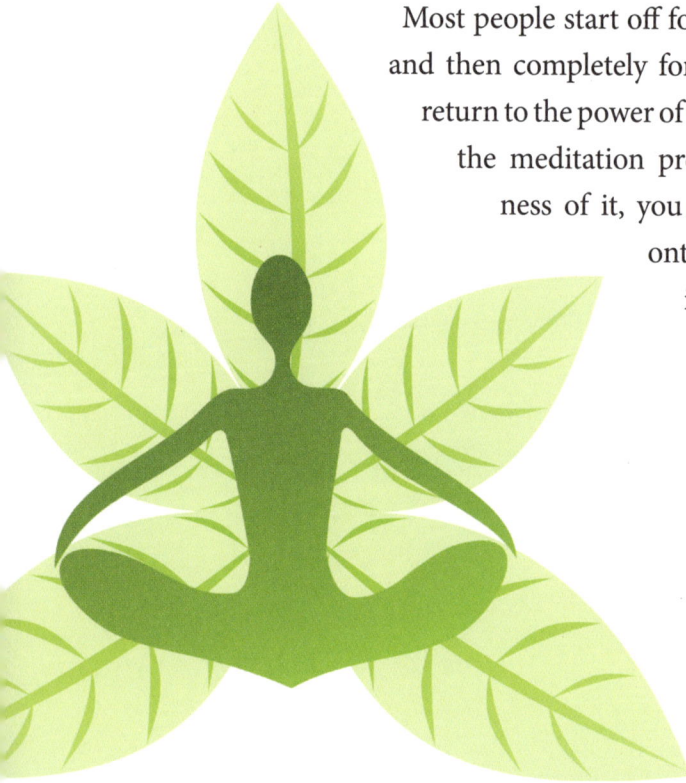

Relax your muscles

Our bodies carry an enormous amount of physical tension. When we walk, we use about two hundred different muscles. Do you remember to release them when you sit or lie down? Probably not. Try the following exercise to bring about awareness of your muscles and teach you how to relax them.

Sit or lie down and close your eyes. Breathe deeply and let yourself relax. You are going to build a system of awareness around your body, rotating your consciousness, allowing yourself to feel the tension in each part and then learning how to release it.

Start with your right foot. Focus on nothing but this foot. Crunch up your toes and feel the tension seeping through the foot and up your leg. Now take a deep breath in and as you breathe out, relax all the muscles. Enjoy the wonderful sensation of the tension leaving this part of you. Breathe in and out again if you can still feel the tension in your right foot.

Repeat this process, working slowly through your entire body from your foot up your leg to your arms on each side, then from your buttocks up to your back and shoulders, your neck, your head and then down to your chest and stomach.

Remember to focus on one part of your body at a time. Take a deep breath in as you tense each part and then as you breathe out, feel the tension ebbing away. Then tense the whole body and relax it. Do this several times.

Now, mentally go through your whole body and ask yourself where tension remains. You can do this quite quickly if you are really focusing. Is your jaw still tight? Release it. Are your shoulders still aching? Release the muscles. Always release on the out breath. Really feel it happen as you exhale.

When you have thoroughly gone through your whole body, lie there quietly for a few minutes, appreciating your newly relaxed, physical body. Notice how much more ready you feel to enter a meditative state. Give yourself a moment to return to reality before you get up and continue your daily life.

Stay hydrated

It is common to find yourself becoming quite dry and thirsty during meditation, particularly as you gradually slip into longer and longer periods of time when you remain still and silent and sink deeper into altered states of consciousness.

As you come out of the meditation and open your eyes, it is a good idea to drink some water, to help rebalance. Often insights come slowly after you have finished; you need some time just to be quiet and digest what you have gleaned. Learn to be gentle with yourself when you finish. Sit for a few minutes silently appreciating what you have learned from your meditation.

Grounding yourself

Sometimes you may find it hard to return to earth after a meditation. You might feel as though your head is still up in the clouds; although it's a wonderful feeling, you need to continue with your day. This process of returning to earth is also called grounding yourself.

You know that focusing on your breathing can always help ground you again, but focusing on your feet is another effective way of returning to reality after your levels of consciousness have been resting elsewhere. Just make sure that you keep breathing deeply as you do the following grounding exercise.

TRY THIS

✻ Close your eyes and focus on your feet. (If you choose to meditate lying down, bend your legs so that the soles of your feet are resting flat on the floor. If you are sitting, make sure your legs are not crossed and that your feet are resting flat on the floor.) As you concentrate, realize how heavy your feet feel. They seem to be like lead, solid and secure on the floor. It would be hard for you to lift them.

✻ Now imagine that the soles of your feet have long roots growing out of them and that these roots are anchored deep into the earth below you. Feel the roots coming out of your feet and going deep into the ground.

✻ As you focus on your feet, you will slowly feel yourself sinking back into your whole body again. You will become aware that all of you feels comfortably heavy and relaxed. Notice which parts of you are touching the floor, chair, or bed and realize how solid they feel.

✻ Focus on your breathing again as you open your eyes. Become aware of how different you feel now that you're grounded. Wait a moment before you get up.

Part Four
Finding Inner Calm

"Feel a wonderful
golden hue spreading
slowly through every
part of you."

Going into the stillness

For most of us, our normal state is to be thinking about a number of different issues all at once. This chapter shows you how to find your stillness—a wonderfully quiet, peaceful place that you will go to each and every time you meditate. Try the breathing technique below to help you begin the process.

IN AND OUT MEDITATION

✳ Close your eyes and focus on your breathing. Initially, you just want to observe the breath, nothing more. Settle yourself and give yourself time to focus. If you want to go into your cleansing sanctuary and get rid of anything unwanted, or if you want to use your own personal technique to stop other thoughts and emotions from distracting you, that is fine.

✳ Now, as you focus on your breathing you are going to use two simple words to increase your focus. Every time you breathe in, say silently to yourself "in." Every time you breathe out, say silently to yourself "out." Keep doing this. Say "in." Say "out." Every time another thought comes into your head, other than these two simple words, acknowledge it then immediately dismiss it. Let it drift away into nothingness. Nothing exists beyond the words "in" and "out." Keep concentrating for several minutes.

✳ As you do so, notice how your breathing is changing. It is deepening and slowing down. Notice how much slower and how much more of a gap there is between your saying "in" and "out." Take your time as you do this. Keep letting other thoughts drift away. Don't hold on to anything except "in" and "out."

✳ When you are ready, slowly open your eyes and take some time to focus on an object and reorient yourself. Sip your water and sit quietly for a few minutes.

Playing with numbers

This is another great exercise to help still your mind and improve your concentration.

Close your eyes and focus on your breathing. Acknowledge each breath coming in and going out. Give yourself a few minutes to settle comfortably.

Now when you next breathe in, say "one." As you breathe out, say "one." Breathe in again and say "two." Breathe out and say "two." Continue this process. If you get confused and aren't sure which number you are on, return to one and start again. When you successfully get to twenty, stop counting.

Now you are going to start again, but this time you want only to think of the number you are currently using. Can you focus solely on the number you are saying, without having your thoughts travel on to the next number or the number you have just said? Can you regard each number as a number and not give it any other significance? This isn't as easy as it sounds! Try it for yourself.

KEEP YOUR FOCUS

The only rule is that you must focus just on the number itself as you breathe in and out; nothing else is allowed to come into your mind. Every time another thought or number comes into your mind, start again at one. You can vary the way you play with numbers. You can start with any number you like and count backwards. Pick a random number such as 87 and count backwards from it. See how far you can get. Return to the same number and start again when you have to. You can start at another random number and work your way upwards. Choose a high number, such as 999. Keep focusing on different numbers that will test your ability to concentrate.

THE CANDLE MEDITATION

A simple candle flame can help you work toward discovering the center of stillness inside you.

✳ Place a lit candle comfortably in your line of sight, directly in front of you.

✳ Now close your eyes and spend a moment or two focusing on your breathing. When you feel relaxed and ready, open your eyes and let your focus rest on the candle flame.

✳ Just gaze gently at the flame. Acknowledge its beauty. Lose yourself in the flame. Let your gaze soften and blur slightly. Feel your awareness melt into the flickering flame itself.

✳ Focus on nothing but the flame and feel as though you are part of it and it is part of you. You might want to let your eyes close as you do this; you will still see the flickering flame in your mind's eye. If you

feel the flame is starting to fade, open your eyes again and focus on it for a while.

✳ Now allow your awareness of the beauty and warmth of the flame to come into your own body. Imagine this soft, comforting flame coming slowly into the area of your heart. Feel it warm and enrich you.

✳ When you are ready, let yourself feel its glow expanding and filling you. See or sense its wonderful golden hue spreading slowly through every part of you, making you feel warm, relaxed, safe and contented. Enjoy the sensation of peace that comes with it. Everything is all right in your world. Enjoy that knowledge.

✳ After a few minutes, see the flame withdraw from your body, leaving you with the comforting sensation of a wonderful, warm glow inside. Realize the flickering flame is in front of you on top of the candle. Slowly open your eyes and focus on the flame. Give silent thanks for its unique beauty.

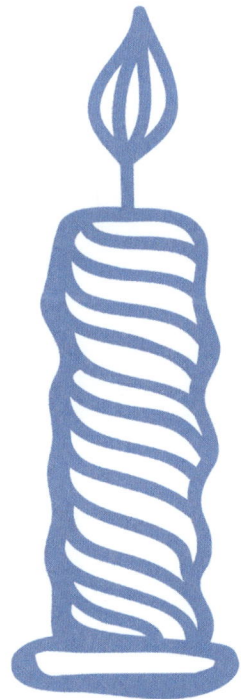

FLOWER MEDITATION

❊ Place a beautiful single flower, in water, in front of you. Now close your eyes and relax, using the technique you find most helpful. Work with your breathing and feel it deepen and slow down. When you're ready, open your eyes and focus on the flower head.

❊ Really look at it, without straining, and enjoy its wonderful beauty. Realize how special each flower is and what a work of nature flowers are. Enjoy its texture, its color. It may even have a scent you can appreciate. Let yourself be filled with wonder and appreciation for this offering from nature.

❊ Let your consciousness melt into the flower itself. Feel what it is like to be a part of nature. Enjoy this comforting sensation. Be aware of what it really means—to be part of the constant ebb and flow of life in all its cycles and seasons.

❊ When you are ready, close your eyes and bring the consciousness of this magnificent flower into your own body. Feel it melt into your physical being and travel into the heart of you. Enjoy its pulsing softness and beauty. Acknowledge how wonderful it makes you feel and the sense of peace it brings. Wallow in the feeling.

✳ Wait until you feel ready and then let the image of the flower return to the flower in front of you. Withdraw it from your physical body and open your eyes, to see it there in front of you. Give silent thanks for its beauty and to nature, its creator.

✳ Reorient yourself slowly.

You can, of course, put anything symbolic into this exercise. The simpler the image, the more powerful it usually is. Do you have a beautiful seashell that you love? Try meditating on that. A stone, crystal or piece of wood can also be effective.

Going into stillness

This is quite a lengthy exercise that will help you step into the stillness which heralds deeper meditation. Ensure you go through the checklist and then settle into your comfortable position. Read through the exercise first, and when you are ready, begin.

✳ Close your eyes. Wriggle your body gently into a comfortable position. Start observing your breath. Don't alter it in any way. Notice if you are feeling relaxed or tense. Let yourself go into your cleansing sanctuary for a while. Cleanse and renew your energies. Feel yourself melt into a comfortable state of relaxation.

✳ Now return to your breathing. Feel each breath coming in and going out. Use whatever technique you wish to lengthen and deepen the breath, such as the stomach, ribcage or balloon breathing exercises. Try the numbers or use the "in" and "out" technique. Give yourself time to adjust and let the deeper breathing feel natural and unforced.

✳ Now you are going to shift your focus from each in and out breath to another area. You are going to feel your focus going to a point deep within your body—the part of you

that is peaceful, still and quiet. You are going to find this area for yourself. It is hidden deep in the middle of your body, below your ribcage and around your navel area. This is the very center, the very core of you. It is a wonderfully calm, soothing place. You can take your time to find it.

✳ Start by taking your focus from your breathing to the area just below your ribcage. Then let your focus slowly shift from the ribcage to a little further down, toward your belly button. Keep exploring. Take some time to find this area. Give yourself time to find the stillness. There is no rush.

✳ Wait until you can feel the contact. It will probably manifest itself as a slight sensation of something different happening to you. It may be a pleasurable tingle or gentle tickle inside. Perhaps it will feel like a warm glow or a welcome sensation of a cool breeze flowing through you. Everyone feels it differently. Some people even have a scent in their nostrils or hear a beautiful sound such as tinkling bells in the distance. Give yourself time to find out what your natural reaction is to this new world. Don't rush.

✳ Now let yourself sink into this place. It is so inviting, it is easy to do this. Drop slowly into the wonderfully warm, soft enveloping sense of peace. Let yourself really relax into it. Realize how comforted, safe and contented you feel here. Remember to keep your breathing deep and regular. Just let yourself wallow in the pleasure of this new place. Rest here for quite a while. Make a mental note of where this place is in your body, and know you will come here again.

COME BACK TO AWARENESS

Then, when you are ready, withdraw your concentration from this area. Let yourself come back to your breathing and focus on each in and out breath. Focus on your real life again. Slowly bring yourself back to awareness of the present. Notice how heavy your body feels. Slowly open your eyes and focus on an object. Take sip of water and wait a while before you get up.

How did your physical body feel after that experience? You may have felt strange when you first opened your eyes. You may have felt you didn't really find this stillness. You may just have felt relaxed, or maybe you know you didn't find what you were supposed to. Whatever your experience, that is fine.

THE RETREAT MEDITATION

While some techniques work inward into silence, this beautiful meditation starts with an awareness of outer influences.

✳ Start off by settling yourself comfortably into your meditating position. Close your eyes, and relax into your deeper breathing.

✳ Now you want to take your awareness to outside sounds. Really listen to see what you can hear outside. Can you hear a plane flying? Perhaps birds are twittering in the trees. Perhaps you can hear people walking down the street chatting. Whatever you hear, try to identify it and then let it fade from your consciousness. Make sure you have fully identified all the distant sounds you can hear.

✳ Now move a little closer to your own surroundings. What can you hear just outside the room you are in? Is there the hum of electrical appliances? Are floorboards creaking or is there a whirr of heating or air conditioning? Maybe you can hear a pet moving around the house or even snoring. Really listen to the sounds outside your room. As soon as you recognize them, let them float away.

✳ Now bring your focus to the room you are in. What sounds can you hear in the room itself? Is there the ticking of a clock? Perhaps a breeze is blowing through the window. Again, listen intently to anything you can identify within the room itself, but try not to hold on to the awareness of the sound. Let it fade away.

✳ Now start to bring your awareness closer to you, just around your body itself. Become aware of the space your physical body occupies and tune in to that. What can you hear? What is that new sound you now hear? Focus. If you listen closely enough you will hear it. It is a gentle, repetitious thudding sound, faint but persistent. Can you hear it?

✳ It is your heartbeat. Listen to it. Enjoy it. This is your very life source, work your body does day in, day out, to keep you alive and healthy. Appreciate the sound. Really become aware of it. Move your awareness within your own body to access its center. Take a journey into your heart area and appreciate the strength and beauty residing there.

✳ As you move inside, be aware of other sounds inside your body. Can you hear your stomach gurgling as its digests? Can you feel your veins pulsing gently in other parts of your body? Realize what a powerhouse of activity takes place constantly in your own body. Give silent thanks for its divine existence.

THE SOUND OF SILENCE

Now move deeper, into the very core of your body. Can you find an area that is deep, dark, silent and still? Gently explore with your conscious thought. As you do so, let the other sounds in your body fade into the distance. Gradually become aware that there are no more sounds. No sounds remain. Only silence. There is only wonderful silence—pure, clear silence that is infinitely comforting and peaceful. Nothing exists here but stillness and a wonderful sense of nothingness. Rest in this absolute silence and stillness for as long as you like. If any thoughts come into your head, let them fade away. Enjoy the sensation of nothingness. Savor it.

Then, very slowly, bring your awareness back to the everyday sounds around you. Realize that the clock is ticking. You can hear the wind in the trees or the rain on the window. Really focus on everyday sounds again. Gently open your eyes and focus on the room you are in. Sip your water. Take your time to return to the present day.

Part Five
Sounds and Scents

"The power of a mantra
lies in your ability to
lose yourself in its rich,
sonorous sound."

Discovering mantras

The sounds we can make ourselves have long been used in meditating. Making a sound and repeating it constantly is known as a "mantra." Most ancient forms of meditation use mantras, as indeed do many of the more modern, Western forms of meditation, which regard them as the main method through which inner calm can be discovered.

Because making a strange noise and continuously repeating it might feel odd to you, it is doubly important for this type of meditation that you are in a quiet place, and will not be disturbed. You might also want to ensure that no one else is within earshot.

First, choose a sound and then, breathing deeply and comfortably, utter that sound out loud, slowly and sonorously. The sound will last as long as your breath. Stop only to refill your lungs and then continue. Does it feel strange to you? Perhaps you are wondering how this can possibly be a powerful experience.

HUM A TUNE

Now try something else. Take a comfortable, deep breath and then hum a low note quietly to yourself. Pitch the note near the bottom of your register so that it resonates inside you. How does that feel in your body? Can you feel a sort of tingle or vibration deep inside? Take another deep breath and quietly hum a high note near the top of your register. How different is that as a sensation in your body? Did you notice different parts of your body reacting to each note? Did you find the high note or the low note more comfortable?

For meditative purposes, it is accepted that a lower note is more in harmony with your body and that it is easier to relax with a lower note than a high, piercing one. So, besides choosing your lower register, what else do you need to create an effective mantra?

SIMPLE SOUNDS

First, it's better not to use a real word. Although some words, such as "peace" or "calm," might sound comforting, the problem is that you may be tempted to think about their meaning and what the words mean to you. The purpose and power of a mantra lies in your ability to lose yourself in its rich, sonorous sound and the way it vibrates around and through your body. If you are thinking consciously or unconsciously about the word, it stops the mantra from doing its job.

A mantra should be no more than one or two syllables. It is the simplicity of the sound that will help you focus. You

want something you can repeat continuously without effort and conscious thought.

Certain consonants are more helpful than others for meditating. Let's do another experiment to help prove this. Quietly utter the "s" sound to yourself. Now say the "n" sound softly to yourself. Which feels richer and vibrates more? Try saying the "t" sound. Now say the "w" sound. You'll probably agree that the "n" and "w" sounds vibrate through you. The "t" and "s" sounds seem sharper, higher and less resonant.

So, you want to find a word that has no recognizable meaning, that has only one or two syllables and that consists of consonants which resonate in a rich, comforting way in and around your body. Creating a mantra is a very personal matter, so it is good if you can discover your own word.

Suggested mantras

You may want to choose one of the following, or use one of them as a guideline. You may want to put two of the syllables together.

MAH - NUM	SOHM	DA - YAM
VO - HUM	WONE	RAH - MAH
RAHM	VEE - NONG	SHAH - LOON
LAH - NEE	PRAH	

There are many others you can create. Choose another sound altogether if it feels right for you. The only way to know which sound works for you is to try them all or create your own while in a relaxed state. When you are ready, work through the following exercise.

THE MANTRA MEDITATION

❋ Choose the word you will concentrate on and then close your eyes. Use your cleansing and breathing techniques and allow yourself to sink into a comfortably relaxed state.

❋ Now see your word in your mind's eye. How does it look to you? How does the word make you feel? Take a deep breath and speak it slowly and sonorously to yourself. It can be spoken quite softly if you like. Let the word continue until you have finished the breath. If there are two syllables, try to balance them out equally in your breath, although you may find this difficult at first. Just keep making the sound until your breath runs out. Then take a deep breath in and repeat the process. Do this at least three times with the word.

❋ Notice what feelings and sensations come to you at this time. Where do you feel the vibrations in your body?

❋ Really feel the word vibrate through and around you. Lose yourself in the word completely. Feel it spread outwards from you in a wonderful glow of energy. Let yourself merge with the sound and then become nothing but the sound itself. You will find that you are unaware when you are breathing in because the sound seems continuous as its vibrations spread ever wider and intensify. Stay in this state for some time.

DISCOVER YOUR WORD

When you are ready, slowly prepare to withdraw from your word. To do this, start chanting the word more slowly and more quietly. Gradually, make it softer and softer. Let it gently fade into nothingness. If this has been powerful for you, then you may find it difficult to let the vibrations of the sound disappear. Give yourself some time for this to happen. Cleanse it away if you need to. Don't rush the process.

Let yourself sit in the stillness for a while. Enjoy the silence. Now you might want to discover if there is a mantra out there for you which is personal and right for you. Focus on this possibility. Ask for help. Say you would like to be given your own private mantra that will work powerfully for you. See if anything comes to you. Sit quietly and wait with your eyes closed. Keep concentrating on the possibility of there being a word that is meant just for you and that will be revealed in your state of higher awareness.

When you open your eyes, you may find that the room suddenly feels very bright and clear. It may seem as though it is pulsating with light. You may notice you are tingling with a vibrant energy you haven't felt before. Be sure to give yourself plenty of time to readjust again. Sip your water very slowly. Sit quietly for five minutes before you get up.

Using other sounds

There are some other sounds you might choose to have around you while you meditate. It does not have to be you making the sound; it can be an external force. You might prefer to focus on your breathing and let other sounds wash over you without you having to actually make them.

So, if you choose an outside sound, what might you enjoy and find soothing? This is, of course, very personal; you will have to experiment and see what works for you.

Now is your chance to learn about which sounds you find therapeutic. Let's start with sounds of nature. Do you like the sound of the wind rustling the leaves of trees? Perhaps waves pounding on a seashore or the rush of a powerful waterfall make you feel good. Birdsong can be wonderfully uplifting and relaxing.

SHAKE IT UP

There are plenty of man-made sounds as well. What about drums beating or rattles shaking? These are used in many Indian and Shamanic practices. The ringing of bells is used by Buddhists to bring about awareness. You might prefer the sound of flutes or harps.

During your meditations, try experimenting with different types of sounds and see what works. Buy a small wind chime and place it in a breeze by a window. See what that feels like to you. You can even get a

glass jar, fill it with dried beans and shake it. What does that sound feel like to you? If you like it, why don't you record it onto your phone and play it back.

You may be surprised that certain noises really are helpful and comforting. Let yourself enjoy the learning process of sound and its effects, and take your time. There is always some new sound for you to experiment with.

The power of scent

Appreciation of scents has existed since early man. Aromatherapy, the art of using essential oils to nurture and balance our energy system, is one of the most ancient forms of healing, while flowers and incense can also be incredibly beneficial.

So what scents are going to be helpful to you? Now is the time for you to start experimenting.

Certain flowers have very powerful odors; which ones do you like? Make a habit of sniffing the flowers you come across. This is another wonderful way of living your life in daily awareness. When you stop and smell a flower, it's impossible not to be filled with appreciation for its beauty.

If the area in which you live is barren flower-wise, then notice what trees you have around you and, when they bloom, stop and smell their flowers. You can also go into florist shops or stop and study the flowers at the farmer's market. Certain flowers, such as freesias and lilies, have very strong aromas that can

fill a small room with a glorious scent. Do you like the sweet perfume of lilies? Perhaps you prefer the delicate scent of roses.

When you next take a walk in a park or forest, stop and smell the plants. Certain houseplants—scented geraniums, for example—can make wonderful additions to your meditation room. Simply brush your hand delicately across a geranium and the scent will linger on your skin. Give yourself time to experience this new appreciation of the world of scent.

Flowers and plants

Certain flowers are said to have specific purposes and produce particular effects. This does not mean that you will necessarily respond in the way suggested to all of them, but it might be useful for you to try some of the scents listed below and note your reactions to them.

TRY THESE

✳ **Apple blossom:** divination; health and romance

✳ **Carnation:** self love; physical passion

✳ **Garlic:** protection; health

✳ **Scented geranium:** affirming appreciation of life

✳ **Goldenrod:** protection

✳ **Honeysuckle:** youth

✳ **Hyacinth:** gentleness; femininity

✳ **Jasmine:** self-esteem; psychic development; dreamwork

✳ **Lavender:** inner guidance; spiritual contact

✳ **Lilac:** travel; past lives

✳ **Lily:** spiritual love; purity

✳ **Rose:** awareness of the heart and love; beauty

Essential oils

These precious oils are also a wonderful way to enhance your appreciation of smell when you meditate. Put a few drops in an incense burner or in your bathwater and make a note of how you react to different aromas. Really observe how your meditations differ when you try different oils, as all of them have different properties. Do some make you want to meditate on different areas of your life? Is there a specific feeling that always comes over you when you use a particular oil?

There are also oils you should avoid in certain circumstances, such as pregnancy. If in doubt, always consult with the shop before purchasing one. Never put pure essential oils directly onto your skin; they are too powerful and can cause irritation. Also make sure you buy high-quality oils that only contain the pure essence.

TRY THESE

✳ **Cedarwood:** enhances connection to spirit

✳ **Chamomile:** for inner peace

✳ **Clary sage:** balances the mind and emotions

✳ **Eucalyptus:** clears negativity

✳ **Lemon:** increases energy and encourages clarity

✳ **Marjoram:** calms an agitated mind

✳ **Neroli:** opens the heart and enhances creativity

✳ **Rosemary:** helps increase spiritual awareness

✳ **Rosewood:** enhances meditation

✳ **Vetiver:** aids stillness (known as the "oil of tranquility")

Keep a scent and smell diary

When you have sampled all the flowers, plants and essences around you, turn your attention to different kinds of incense. Fortunately, many shops sell individual incense sticks, giving you the opportunity to try a variety of scents without spending a lot of money. Buy just one or two and burn them in your room as you meditate. Notice what happens and which scents you react favorably to and which make you feel uncomfortable. You might find it useful to keep a scent diary, to monitor your reaction to these new odors.

If you find that you're responding positively to different scents, you might consider investing a little more and working with more advanced concoctions. A good health food or new age shop will be able to provide you with incense sticks that have been specially prepared with natural odors known to enhance meditation.

Notice what happens, which scents you react favorably to, and which make you feel uncomfortable.

TRY DIFFERENT COMBOS

As you continue with your meditations, also continue developing your relationship with sounds and smells, as this will increase your ability to sink into your newly discovered world of stillness and peace. Really work at finding your perfect combinations. You might find it useful to keep a scent and smell diary, to monitor your reaction to these new combinations.

Perhaps it is birdsong in the background with vetiver essence around you. Maybe you prefer harp music and the smell of lilies.

Keep being aware on a daily basis of what is really happening to you and allow yourself to use sounds and smells as helpful balancing tools. Continue using these new tools of awareness as complements to all the new techniques you are about to explore.

What's in a word?

Focusing on a simple word once we are in our meditative state can help our thoughts reach new levels. You have already discovered how a word in the form of a mantra might help you. Now we are going to look at known words and see how awareness of something we recognize can take on a greater level of significance when we are meditating.

Do you often feel that you don't understand the true significance of words, that they elude you in a maddeningly abstract way? This can be true of even relatively simple words you think you ought to know, such as "peace" or "stillness." We are going to continue using words as a wonderful means of showing you what else you can learn about yourself and others. Spend a little time meditating on some of the words listed below and see what each one tells you about aspects of life.

WORDS FOR MEDITATION

Peace	Power	Infinity
Stillness	Conscience	Fate
Cosmos	Life	Time
Truth	Universe	Duality
Honesty	Purpose	Knowledge
Happiness	Destiny	Love
Money	Meditation	

No doubt you can think of words of your own and add them to the list. Make sure that when you meditate, you take yourself fully into that state of stillness before you continue. You might like to write your chosen word in large letters on a piece of paper and prop it up in front of you. Whenever you feel lost or stuck, you can open your eyes and look at the word for fresh inspiration.

WORD MEDITATION

During these meditations you might find it helpful to keep a word diary, as some of what we meditate on can be lost to our conscious memory shortly after we finish meditating.

✳ Close your eyes and settle yourself comfortably. Relax, breathe deeply and let yourself enter your inner stillness. Rest there for a moment and then, when you are ready, open your eyes and look at your chosen word.

✳ What is the first thought that comes into your head? Ask yourself why this is your response. See if a personal experience has triggered this reaction. Then let the feeling drift away. Say the word out loud or say it silently to yourself. Do certain images or sensations come with it? Let yourself flow with those reactions, but try not to become deeply involved with any of them. If you have feelings you don't want, remember to keep washing them away.

✳ Let yourself play with the word. Have it dance it front of you. Have it become bold print, or capitals, or a beautifully flowing scroll. Bounce the word up and down like a ball. Sniff it. Eat it! You are free to respond however you wish. No one will know.

✳ Now make the word become more personal to you. Where does this word manifest itself in your life? Where might you like it to be? What would you have to do to make this happen?

✳ When you are ready, withdraw from the word. If it has really come alive for you during the meditation, you may find it difficult to let the word go. Use your cleansing techniques to get rid of it. Burn it, wash it away, watch it float upwards in a balloon—whatever is powerful for you. Cleanse yourself again before you open your eyes.

Everyday meditations

The technique of using a single word to let your mind spiral onto other levels can also work in improving your toleration of mundane jobs. Are you struggling with the dishes, or a work report, or the routine of picking up the children from school? Whatever you want to give extra meaning to, simply meditate on the action.

At this stage, it is probably easier if you use one word or two to identify the action, such as "work report" or "dishes." If you try to complicate it with long sentences you are going to be throwing a lot of emotions into the meditation, and any insights you receive may be confused and jumbled as a result. To create powerful and helpful meditations, you need to make the concept you are meditating on as simple as possible.

If you are meditating on a personal subject, and are struggling with it for whatever reason, remember that you will have to keep putting aside your own negative feelings during the meditation. If it is an emotional issue for you, then it is natural that your own emotions will be uppermost as you start. This is where the cleansing techniques become so valuable.

TRUE WISDOM

You will discover that it is your own preconceived thoughts about how everything ought to be that get in the way of you moving past the ordinary and progressing into the layers of deep subconscious thought, which is where our true wisdom and knowledge lies. Meditation teaches us just how human we are, and how our individual traits can sometimes stop us from achieving greater awareness.

We have to embrace our human behavior before we can move past it to the higher levels. That's why you are constantly being reminded about awareness of everyday matters and how to bring this into your meditations. By truly embracing our very human responses to everything, we can learn how to let go of them during meditation and understand life on a much deeper level.

Spend time assessing your everyday life through meditation. See what insights come to you by meditating on very simple words such as those below: There are probably quite a few of your own words that you want to add to this list, so feel free to do so!

DAILY WORDS

Washing	Marriage	Mortgage
Cleaning	Partner	Rent
Ironing	Child	Home
Cooking	Parent	Garden
Career	Sibling	Carer

Let yourself enjoy the experience of meditating with each word and notice what insights come to you. Do you find you are developing the ability to view areas of your life in a different way? Of course, some areas will always seem more challenging and frustrating than others. When these crop up, don't worry. If nothing really helpful or insightful happens in an area where you desperately want to understand more, let the emotions wash away and know that shortly you are going to learn some more techniques to help you deal with the heavier issues.

Using visual images

In this section, we're going to be looking at different visual images and assessing what impact they have on you. We're talking about physical images now, not the sort you create in your imagination, although, as you will discover, one can directly affect the other.

Just as you have been discovering what you truly feel about different sounds and smells, now is the opportunity for you to find out what visual images you find helpful and enlightening.

CHOOSING AN IMAGE

First, you are going to consider what visual images help you to relax into a meditative state. After that, we will look at different, more complex images that may help you once you are in a meditative state.

We will begin by thinking about what images you find relaxing. Just as with mantras, you don't want to find yourself getting too distracted by the meaning of the image. If there are people in your image, chances are you will start thinking about what is happening to those people. The simpler and more appealing the image is, the better. A small crystal, a vase of flowers, a picture of the sea, a photo of the moon, a postcard of a tree or other objects of nature.

Relaxing images can also be found in the surface of items that you might have around you already. Have you noticed how beautiful the grain in wood can be? The same is true of a piece of driftwood, a stone or a crystal. A seashell is also an object of enormous intricacy and appeal. Look at a single leaf on a plant. Even the skin on a piece of fruit can be beautiful.

In your daily mindfulness of everything, take time to appreciate what is around you.

Choose your colors

Relaxation in terms of visual images is heavily linked to color; most people find pastel shades much more relaxing than sharp, bright colors. Do the images that soothe you most contain colors that are muted and harmonious together? The color green is known to encourage growth, harmony and loving thoughts; blue is found to have a cooling and calming effect.

Soft pink is also known to have a calming effect, while soft, warm purples are considered beneficial for enhancing spiritual awareness. Are you drawn to any of these colors?

If you have only chosen bright reds and fiery oranges so far, carefully consider whether they will actually soothe you for meditation. This is not to say that you are wrong for choosing them; you might have found the picture of a setting sun painted in rich reds and oranges to be the most inspirational image for you.

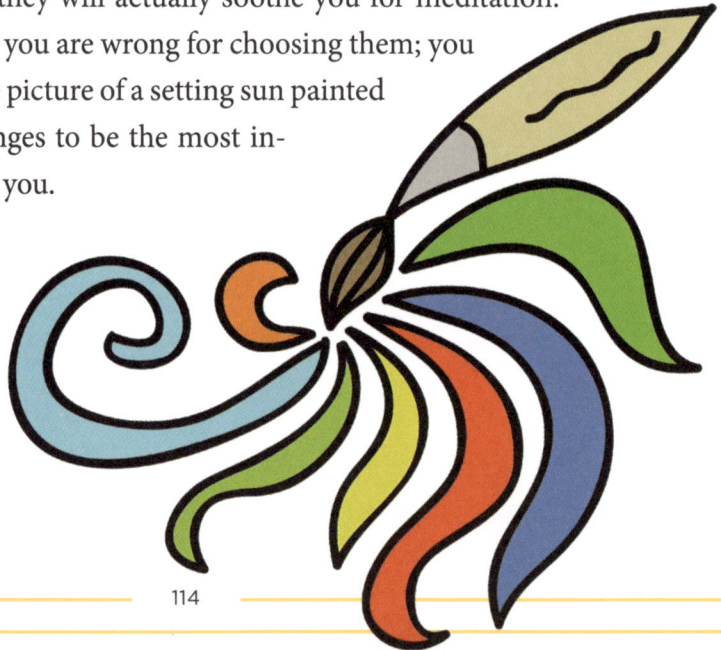

VISUAL MEDITATION

✳ When you have chosen your image, start by relaxing and concentrating on your breathing. You might want to close your eyes while you do this. You don't have to wait until you enter into your inner stillness, because you are going to let the visual image do this for you; just make sure you are relaxed and comfortable first.

✳ Now open your eyes and let your gaze rest on the image or object you have chosen. Don't stare at it; let your gaze be soft and slightly hazy. If you find thoughts coming into your head, keep washing them away. You don't need them now. Empty yourself of responses to what is in front of you. Just let it rest there without judgment or meaning. This is all you have to do. Simply enjoy its beauty.

✳ As you keep your eyes focused on the image or object, notice that it seems to be coming nearer. It may feel as though it is becoming part of you or that you are approaching it and merging; it doesn't matter which.

✳ Let your consciousness slip slowly into the image. Feel yourself slide down into the swirls of the wood or the petals of the flower or the intricate design of the shell or

beauty of the object in front of you. This may
be a gradual process, and may take a long time,
or you may feel swept away on a wonderful
wave of awareness. Whatever happens for you,
it is right.

YOUR MIND'S EYE

As this happens, you may find your eyes closing. You will
find yourself sinking comfortably into your familiar world
of peace and quiet, your private inner core. Let yourself
slide quickly and easily into this state. You may notice that
your image or object has come with you and is still visible
in your mind's eye.

Ask silently why it has come with you into your inner
world of silence and retreat. Find out what you are supposed
to learn from its presence. Spend some time together and
enjoy its comforting presence. Let any pictures or sensations come and go in waves of awareness. Don't try to hold
onto anything. Rest there for as long as it feels right for you.

Then slowly withdraw. Come back to your everyday
world gradually, releasing the image or object from your
mind's eye as you do so. Use your cleansing methods to
get rid of everything you don't want. Wait until you are
properly grounded again before you continue.

Part Six

Working with Energy

"Everything we say and do
gives off a subtle energy."

Your aura

You know something about your physical body and what it can do, but have you ever thought of yourself as being more than purely physical? In your early stages of meditation, you will no doubt have discovered that this quiet inner core you find inside yourself doesn't actually seem to be a tangible area; it's more of a feeling or sensation that comes over you.

Have you sometimes entered a space and been struck by how pleasant it feels, without any obvious reason for it? Likewise, you can also go into a room and suddenly feel very uneasy, without any obvious physical indication as to why you feel this way. Just as with people, you are immediately drawn to some rooms and you want to return to them, to enjoy the feeling of that space.

FEEL THE POWER

So what are you tapping into when you have these responses? The simple answer is: energy! Everything we say and do gives off a subtle energy, or what we call an aura. If the emotion is very strong, we can actually pick up on it and want to react to it. Think about this in terms of what you sense from other people. Do some people give off comforting energy and others make you immediately feel uncomfortable? When someone is in love, can you sense or almost see a golden glow of pleasure around them? Think about the effect of being around someone who is permanently "on edge" and distraught. Now think of being in the calming influence of a gentle and wise figure who is always smiling. Would you say that you can almost tangibly feel these energies, even though they aren't visible to you in a physical sense?

TUNING IN TO MEDITATION

By learning how to tap into your own and other people's energy, you can learn to understand who you really are. You will need to find a willing and enthusiastic friend to help you explore the energies people give out.

✳ Sit across from each other, just a few feet apart, and close your eyes. Both of you need to take a moment to focus yourselves and to breathe deeply. Both of you should keep your eyes closed throughout the exercise.

✳ Now, one of you chooses to be the Giver and the other the Receiver. The Giver concentrates on a particular emotion, while the Receiver sits quietly and relaxes. The Giver needs time to let the emotion become real and vivid to them. However, the Giver at no time speaks or articulates the emotion, they simply feel it and let it seep out of them in an energetic form towards the Receiver. Make sure to work with strong emotions like anger, peace, joy and sadness.

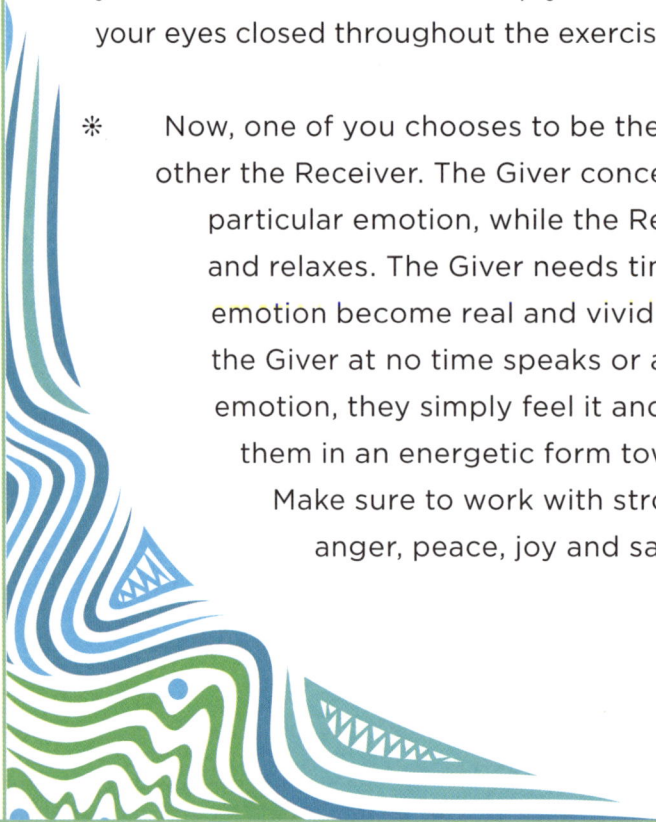

✳ When the Receiver is ready, they
tune in to what is coming at them.
Remembering to keep their eyes closed,
they simply focus on what they feel coming
at them in waves from the Giver. They then
check with the Giver to find out if their feelings
are accurate. Both of you then need to cleanse the
emotion away before you continue.

✳ Try again, or swap over so the Giver becomes the
Receiver, and vice versa. You may find that one person
is more sensitive to picking up energy than the other. The
only rule is that you must remember to cleanse afterwards,
and make sure that the last emotion you choose is a
positive one that leaves you both feeling good.

AURA MEDITATION

N ot all people see auras, although you can train yourself to do so. Try the experiment below one day when you have some uninterrupted time.

* Place a full-length mirror in front of you and a bright white light behind you. Make sure that the area behind you is as dark and plain as possible. It's hard to see auras against patterned backgrounds.

* Now sit or stand quietly in front of the mirror for a few minutes. Focus on your breathing and look inward for a

while, ignoring your own reflection. You might want to close your eyes, but if you're standing up you might find that it makes you feel unbalanced. Calm and still yourself.

✳ When you are ready, open your eyes and focus on the area just around your head. Let your gaze soften; don't stare too hard. Can you see anything? Remember to keep breathing, and don't try too hard. Can you see a vague light? Perhaps it is like a fuzzy white haze or a golden glow. It may encompass the whole head, or only seem to be there in sections. It may seem like the light that a candle flame gives off. You may see nothing at all. Concentrate on the area around your head for a while.

✳ Then let your focus move to other areas around your body. Can you see anything near your heart area? (Like the head, this is another part that can give off and receive powerful energy.) Let your focus shift to different areas of your body and notice when you see something. Don't worry if you can see very little.

✳ When you have finished, remember to wash away anything you didn't like. Take a moment to ground yourself when you have finished.

HAND ENERGY MEDITATION

Y ou might also find it helpful to feel your own aura. Your aura is around all of you at all times; you can't get away from it or separate it in any way from you, so it is always there to work with or play with. A good way to become aware of your energy is to use your hands. Try the next exercise.

✳ Take some deep breaths and relax. Take your time. Now hold your hands up in front of you, palms facing each other, but about eighteen inches apart. Have your fingers straight, but close together rather than spread apart. Now slowly, very, very slowly, move your hands toward each other. Take your time with this; do it gradually and with complete awareness.

✳ Before you get very far, you will feel a slight pulling sensation, as if there is something happening between your hands. You may want to move your hands apart a little. Now move them in again. What can you feel? Slowly, very slowly, move your hands closer and closer together. At some point, you may actually feel like you can't move them any closer together; it may feel as if a force is keeping them apart. This is your own energy, your own aura.

✳ Play with your aura; feel it bounce back and forth between your hands. Try to pat it into a round ball. Let it stretch outwards until you can't feel it, then move it in again. When you have finished, give your hands a good shake and release any restricted energy.

Could you feel that quite strongly? It's a good way to acknowledge that there's some interaction of energy taking place, although you can't actually see it. If you do this exercise again, you may actually be able to see light playing back and forth between your hands.

The layers of the aura

The human aura is known to contain at least seven separate layers of energy, each one becoming finer and lighter in intensity as it radiates outward from the body.

Below is an outline of each of the seven layers of the aura. The first layer is closest to the physical body and is the part that most people initially see when they start focusing on auras. The others radiate outward sequentially.

First layer

The physical self; about being earthed and grounded, enjoying physical activities and pursuits and everything to do with "earthly" living.

Second layer

The emotional self in relation to one's life; about self-expression and self-love.

Third layer

The mental self; to do with rational thoughts and our ability to rationalize.

Fourth layer

Conditional love; how we feel about others and how we relate to them. Here, the energies start to become lighter, finer and harder to see.

Fifth layer

Divine will, the releasing of personal ambitions and emotions; about our ability to see life as part of a larger picture and understand where we fit in.

Sixth layer

Divine love; unconditional and all-encompassing love, allowing us to understand everything in the larger context of universal laws, rather than through earthly attachments.

Seventh layer

Divine mind; about fusing with all spiritual awareness and becoming one with universal truths and laws. Described as a state of bliss.

The chakras

To work on your aura, you first have to discover the door into these layers of energy. These doors are called chakras, the ancient Sanskrit word for "wheel," and their existence has been known for thousands of years.

The seven chakras are basically the entrance into the human aura. They are located at specific parts of the human body. Our body is a complex crisscross of energy lines; it is believed that there are more than seventy-two thousand separate lines of energy running through the human body at all angles. Each of the seven chakras, which are often likened to the petals of a lotus flower, is located at a point where twenty-one lines of energy cross the body.

It is through our increased awareness of the chakras that we can gain access to our auras, and thereby understand a great deal more about the purpose of our life on every level.

You may not have realized it at the time, but when you were meditating on different areas of your life and different issues that have affected you, you were unconsciously tapping into some of these chakras and working with them.

Below is a rundown of each chakra and its significance. You will notice that each chakra relates to each layer of the aura.

Base chakra

Located at the base of the spine, it opens downward, toward the ground. Its associated color is red, and physically it is related to the spinal column, the adrenal glands and the kidneys. This chakra is about your physical sense of being and your appreciation of earthly life, such as love of food, sexual relations and physical activities. It is often called the "root" of you, because it shows how rooted you are in earthly matters. It is also about your instinct for survival, your "flight-or-fight" metabolism.

Navel chakra

This is found just below the navel and opens front and back through the body. Sometimes it is known as the sacral chakra. It is associated with the color orange, and is connected to the reproductive system and our immune system. This is about our sexuality, but not simply referring to the sexual act itself. It deals with how well you form relationships with others, sexual or otherwise. It is about your emotions in relation to this. Given that sexuality is a difficult area for many people, this chakra needs special sensitivity and gentleness.

Solar plexus chakra

This is situated just below the breastbone, slightly to the left. It opens both front and back. The color given is yellow. It is affiliated with the pancreas, stomach, gall bladder, liver and nervous system. This is where you store your mental perception of yourself; it is about self-esteem and how you see yourself fitting into life. It is the seat of your willpower and reflects how you digest information.

Heart chakra

This is found in the middle of the breast-bone and above the chest, and opens both front and back. It is connected to the color green and associated with the thymus gland, heart, blood and circulatory system. This is about love; not just your ability to love yourself and others, but also how you love the universe as a whole. The subtle energies start to change here, and become lighter and finer. The heart chakra is often considered the hinge or link between the physical and spiritual worlds, the point at which true spiritual awareness can start to develop.

Throat chakra

This is located at the hollow of the throat and has two openings, front and back. The color sky blue is connected to this chakra, which relates to the thyroid gland, bronchial tubes and vocal organs, lungs and alimentary canal. This is about how we hear inner truths and learn to speak them.

It reflects what we feel about our professional life too, and how we can expand our awareness on every level. This is about integrity of speech and living through higher awareness.

Brow chakra

Situated in the middle of the forehead, this opens both front and back. Purple is the related color and it's connected to the pituitary gland, lower brain, left eye, ears, nose and nervous system. This is often called our "third eye," and is about our vision—not in a literal sense, but in a much wider, truly spiritual and universal context. As the energies become even finer and higher, these concepts become harder to grasp without actually experiencing them.

Crown chakra

This is found at the very top and center of the head. It has only one opening: upward, toward the sky. It is associated with the color violet, although it is sometimes also referred to as white, since the crown chakra symbolizes purity at all levels of consciousness. The body parts it is connected to are the pineal gland, upper brain and right eye. As this is the highest and finest of all the subtle energies, it is the most difficult to explain. It is related to a state of pure bliss, a sense of understanding and awareness that transcends all earthly words. It is supreme connection and merging with the divine. It is a state to which one can aspire without necessarily understanding all that it encompasses.

Opening your chakras

To consciously open all your chakras, and enjoy the new sensation that comes from this heightened awareness, make sure you follow the usual guidelines. Alternate-nostril breathing is strongly recommended too.

Settle yourself comfortably and close your eyes. Remember to take your time to breathe deeply and relax.

START AT THE BOTTOM OF YOUR SPINE

This is your base chakra. Simply bring your focus to this part of your body. Remember that this chakra only opens downwards, toward the ground, and is never closed. What can you feel? Perhaps you feel a little heaviness in the area, or a pulsing of light or energy. Think of the color red if you like, to help you focus. Now feel how it is moving. Wait until you have acknowledged this chakra before you move on.

MOVE UP TO YOUR BELLY BUTTON

Just below you'll find your navel chakra, which has two openings, front and back, so make sure you focus on both. Can you feel a little tickle as the chakra starts to open? Perhaps it is open already. Can you speed up its vibrations by encouraging it to move a little faster? Focus on the color orange.

UP TO YOUR BREASTBONE

Slightly to the left you'll find your solar plexus chakra. Use the focus of the color yellow to help you. Remember, this chakra opens both front and back. Give yourself time to feel it opening. Every chakra feels different, so don't worry if there is no repeated sensation when you concentrate on each chakra. Just let yourself feel whatever is happening, without judging.

ON TO YOUR HEART

Your heart chakra is where the energies start to change, and become finer and brighter. Focus on your heart area and remember that this chakra opens front and back. Try to balance the flow between the two. Let the color green come into your conscious thought, and feel it flowing through the heart chakra.

THE HOLLOW OF YOUR THROAT

Concentrate here on the throat chakra. Feel it opening front and back. Notice if the feeling makes you want to swallow or clear your throat. Focus on the blue color of a clear sky.

MOVE UP TO YOUR FOREHEAD

The spot in the middle is the brow chakra. Feel it opening front and back. Bring the color purple into this area and see how that affects the chakra opening. The brow chakra is called the "third eye" by clairvoyants, who focus on it to attain higher energies.

THE CROWN CHAKRA

Finally, move to the top and middle of your head. This has only one opening: upward, toward the sky. It is always open, but you want to feel it open a little more. Focus on it and notice what you feel. The crown chakra seems to be powerful on physical as well as etheric levels.

CLEANSE YOUR AURA

Lastly, let yourself slip into your cleansing sanctuary, and cleanse your whole aura by letting the water or light come down through each chakra, starting with the crown, and gently washing away anything you don't want. Take this process very slowly, and enjoy it. Carefully go through each chakra in reverse: crown, brow, throat, heart, solar plexus, navel and base. Enjoy the sensation of all your energies feeling more alive and receptive to everything around you, both physically and spiritually.

CLOSING YOUR CHAKRAS MEDITATION

Opening up can be a wonderful sensation, but it's essential to learn how to close down properly, so you're grounded before you continue in the everyday world.

❋ Cleanse by using your usual technique. Feel anything you don't want being washed away with your light or water. You want to make sure that nothing unpleasant remains in your energy field before you close your chakras.

❋ Now, starting with the base chakra, feel the chakra gently slowing down under your focus. Remember, this chakra always stays open to a certain extent, but it will have become much more active during your concentration. Feel it gradually slowing down. You will still sense it pulsing or moving slightly, but know it is now moving in a gentle, less energetic way.

❋ Move up to the navel chakra. Concentrate on this area and feel the chakra slowly close, both front and back. It is useful to create your own image for this, to make the action more powerful. Imagine the petals of a flower folding, a door closing, or whatever works best for you.

✳ Continue this process up through the solar plexus, heart,
throat and brow, remembering to close each chakra both
front and back. When you reach the crown, remember that
this chakra stays open at all times, but you want to slow
down its energies. Feel it pulsing at a lower rate or shining
less brightly.

Sometimes, after closing your chakras, you can still feel slightly lighthead-
ed from your new state of awareness. Remember to use your grounding
energy exercise and focus on your feet. Notice how heavy your body feels
in the chair. Always use this as a grounding tool before you get up again
when you are working consciously with your chakras.

CLOAK OF PROTECTION MEDITATION

This effective technique will help you feel more secure after a sensitive meditation. You can use it any time, whether finishing a meditation, stuck on a crowded bus or train, or feeling bombarded by someone else's energies.

You're going to create your own invisible cloak of protection that you can call on at any time to wrap around you.

✳ Sit quietly and close your eyes. Breathe deeply. Let yourself settle and become still. Slip into the state of inner silence that you love and are beginning to know well. Sit quietly for a few minutes.

✳ Now, silently ask that you be given your own personal cloak of protection. Wait a little while. Don't expect instant results. Gradually, something will be shown to you. You will see it, feel it or sense it. It is your own personal cloak of protection, so it will be something that is right and powerful for you. It may come in the form of brilliant light that surrounds you and gives you a feeling of safety. You may be given shimmering armor, or a fabric that's waterproof and warm.

FEEL SAFE

Whatever you put on, it should immediately make you feel good. You shouldn't feel heavy, restricted or claustrophobic. It may not have any earthly connection, so it may be a sensation rather than a physical image for you. All that matters is that it makes you feel safe and insulated from any unwanted outside influences. This cloak of protection does not shut you off from everyone. You can still give out your energies and receive back what you want to receive. But nothing unwanted can bombard you. Nothing unpleasant can get through.

The cloak of protection is yours forever. Call on it any time you need it, and release it any time you don't.

Part Seven
Free Your Mind

"Breathe into the silence and embrace the sacred stillness."

Freeing meditations

The meditations you will experience in this chapter are designed to free your mind and enable you to relax.

You can experience these meditations in the same way as you have the others: by reading each one first, then closing your eyes and running through them in your mind, remembering as much as you can. However, consider trying something different. Why not record yourself or the voice of a friend reciting the meditation?

It's important to choose someone whose voice you enjoy listening to, not someone whose accent or energy you find difficult or distracting. Your relaxation will come from the content of the meditation and the timbre of the voice of the person who is speaking. The voice should be calm but not monotonous, steady without being too slow, and warm without being syrupy.

REMEMBER THE GUIDELINES

Although these are freeing meditations, you should still take into account all the requirements on your meditation checklist. If you want to test the theory, you might try meditating one day when you don't observe one of the rules. For instance, put on a tight pair of pants and then try to relax into a meditation! There's nothing like experiencing something like this once to make you appreciate why you follow certain guidelines.

The more you revisit these meditations, the more the locations will come alive for you and the more benefit you will receive from them. You will find that the locations expand and become more detailed and vibrant on each visit, as you yourself grow and expand. Different insights will come with each meditation, relevant to what is happening to you at that particular time. However, first and foremost, these remain the most relaxing and comforting of meditations, somewhere you will always feel safe and nurtured.

OPENING RELAXATION MEDITATION

This exercise should be a precursor to every subsequent meditation. It's important to give yourself that initial time to sink into your inner stillness.

✳ Close your eyes and relax. Allow any tension to seep out. This is your time now, time just for you, to be alone, relax and unwind. You are now going to release unwanted pressure from your body. Feel it going from your head ... neck ... shoulders ... arms, hands and fingers ... through your torso and down your legs ... right out through your toes ...

✳ Feel the tension you've been carrying melting away, deep into the ground, becoming nothing.

✳ Now focus on your breathing. Watch it come and go through your body ... Feel as though each breath is being taken deep down into your navel ... Feel each breath as it comes up and out through your nose ... Let your ribcage expand on each breath in; feel it contract as you breathe out. Sit in awareness of your breathing for a few minutes. Observe each breath in and each breath out ...

✳ Whatever problems or anxieties come into your mind, now is the time to let them slip away. Use your cleansing sanctuary to help you ... Say goodbye to them now ... You don't need them ...

✳ Feel yourself sink into your inner core, into the stillness inside of you. Take that journey inwards now, gently, slowly ... Let yourself go ... Relax ... Breathe into the silence, into the sacred stillness ... Now embrace this wonderful sensation of peace and safety ... Feel it running around and through you ... Feel yourself merging with the feeling, so that you and the feeling are one ... Nothing can harm you here ... You are safe ... peaceful ... still ...

GARDEN MEDITATION

This is another excellent relaxation technique to try.

✳ After your Opening Relaxation, find yourself in a garden or yard. This is a beautiful place; it is the garden of your dreams. The grass is soft and warm under your bare feet, the sun is shining and it feels warm and comforting without being too hot. There is a soft, gentle breeze wafting sweet scents toward you. You can recognize various aromas of flowers and shrubs, all mingling together. You can hear birdsong and the light rustle of the wind in the trees. You may hear a trickle of water and realize there is a pond in your garden, or a river.

✳ Explore your garden. Walk around it. See how beautiful it is. Smell everything. Perhaps there's a wild strawberry patch or an apple from a tree that you want to taste. Enjoy the warm sun on your body.

FIND INNER CALM

You find somewhere to rest. Maybe there's a bench in your garden, or a comfy lounge chair, or perhaps you just want to lie on the warm grass. You close your eyes and still feel the garden around you, smell its scents and hear its sounds. You can feel yourself merging with the beauty of the garden, appreciating everything from within.

You are wonderfully relaxed and at peace. Everything is right in your world.

Continue to rest in appreciation and awareness. Feel the nurturing strength and power of the garden around you, blessing all of you: physically, emotionally, mentally and spiritually … Stay in this state for a few minutes longer …

Now it's time for you to withdraw. You have to say goodbye to your garden, but you can return to it any time. You can resolve to return soon.

BEACH MEDITATION

Try this exercise when you want to transport yourself to another location. Remember to do the Opening Relaxation first.

✳ You find yourself on a beautiful deserted beach. There is no one else there. This is your ideal beach. There may be palm trees waving on the beach, or a straw hut. It is wonderfully warm and sunny, just the right temperature for you. There is a cool breeze blowing. The waves are lapping at the shore.

✳ Take a walk and explore your beautiful beach. It is just for you. Walk barefoot and feel the warm sand or smooth rocks under your bare feet. Smell the ozone in the air. You can hear the waves as they fall upon the shore, and the distant cry of sea birds. You can see the sunlight sparkling on the water.

✳ You find out that everything you could possibly need or want is here: a supply of large, dry towels, tanning lotion, drinks, food, sun hat, beach umbrella, spare clothes, perhaps a good book. Maybe there's a soft lounge chair or an inflatable raft to float on in the sea.

FEEL THE POWER OF NATURE

While you're enjoying yourself in your private paradise, you are also appreciating everything around you, acknowledging how beautiful and perfect everything in nature is. You become aware of the special power of the sea and its pull. You merge your energies with the energies of the sea and enjoy its strength.

At some time during your visit, you are also given an inspirational thought that hasn't been given to you before. Give thanks for this new insight. Take it with you when you go.

Now it's time for you to leave. You have to say goodbye to this wonderful beach, but you will be able to return whenever you wish. Know that you will indeed soon revisit this peaceful haven.

FOREST MEDITATION

This is another meditation to bring about inner calm and peace. Again, remember to start with the Opening Relaxation.

* You are walking in a beautiful forest. This is not a thick, dense forest; it is open and light, with lots of sunshine. There are different beautiful trees around you and the sun is shining brightly through them, leaving dappled images on the soft ground beneath your feet. There is a gentle breeze blowing.

* Walk slowly through this amazing place. You have never seen so many trees before, a variety of species, heights, colors and shapes. The scents coming from them are wonderful. You can hear the rustling of the leaves and the songs of various birds as they fly through this beautiful forest. There is a humming of different insects as they pass busily by. Perhaps you see a monkey or other wildlife in the distance, enjoying the bounty of the trees. The ground feels soft and warm under your bare feet.

NURTURING TREE ENERGY

You feel the beauty and power of the trees coming into you and nurturing your energies. After a while, you decide to sit down in a clearing in the sunshine. You rest in the middle of the forest, looking up at all the beautiful trees around you. As you sit there, you suddenly receive a flash of higher awareness, a greater understanding about some element of life that had previously eluded you. You wonder why you had not realized this before. You sit in the joy of discovering this new truth, and give thanks for it having come forward into your conscious mind.

Now it's time for you to leave. You have to go from this wonderful forest, but you will return another day. You know that you will want to come back soon to continue exploring these inspirational trees.

YOUR ANGEL OF FUN MEDITATION

Let's finish with a light and enjoyable meditation that encourages us to remember the lighter qualities we possess.

✳ Close your eyes and settle into a comfortable position. Feel your body unwinding.

✳ As you do this, realize that a wonderful energy has just entered into your awareness. This is a light, frothy energy, unlike any of the others you've experienced. This energy is bright and instantly uplifting. You may see a sprightly figure as this happens, or just hear, sense or smell in your own way.

✳ It dances around and through you, making you want to laugh, making you want to smile. You feel yourself relax in the company of this new energy.

✳ This is your angel of fun; they have come to lighten and brighten your day. Observe what they do. They may clown around or joke and make you laugh. They may just dance in front of you. Perhaps they are singing.

✳ They may be showing you something that you could introduce into your own life to enjoy it more. Observe what they do without judging them. You might think they are silly; you might find them enchanting. It doesn't matter what you think of them, as long as you enjoy their presence.

HARNESS YOUR INNATE JOY

Angels of fun are a delightful boost to our everyday life and can give us a much-needed injection of optimism and pleasure. Do you have an important business meeting coming up, or are you dreading seeing someone who always gives you a hard time? Lighten your energy by inviting your angel of fun to visit you, even for a few minutes.

Final thoughts

Meditation is not about escaping from the reality of our earthly existence; it is about helping us live more harmoniously within it. This means finding out how to improve every facet of our lives on an emotional, mental, physical and spiritual level. When you meditate, you are not being indulgent and spoiling yourself; you are actually facilitating the very process of living.

If you are struggling to find enough time to meditate on a regular basis, when you have an opportunity, try meditating on the word "meditation." This will give you a chance to rediscover what meditation really means and strengthen your relationship with it.

Finally, there is one tool that will help you solve or find your way through any difficulty you have with meditation: the breath. No matter how often you have had the importance of breathing stressed to you, no matter how often you have been told to breathe, it cannot be enough. We all keep forgetting to stop and breathe deeply—and yet, when we do, the results are immediately apparent.

Whatever difficulty you encounter any time before, during and after meditation, the secret to unlocking the difficulty will always be to breathe into it.

You are the true master of your own destiny. Decide that you will enjoy this process called life. See it not as something you have to get through, but as a moment in time to be treasured, relished and enjoyed to the full.

Closing prayer

Divine Light,

Help me to see the way forward with love, light and joy.

Show me how best to help others, as well as myself.

Let me spread your Divine Light through myself and others

without judgment, conditions or expectations.

Amen.

Mindfulness

Mindfulness

How to pay attention
to the present

Wendy Hobson

SIRIUS

All illustrations courtesy of Shutterstock.

SIRIUS

This edition published in 2021 by Sirius Publishing, a division of
Arcturus Publishing Limited,
26/27 Bickels Yard, 151–153 Bermondsey Street,
London SE1 3HA

ISBN: 978-1-3988-1318-2
AD007323US

Printed in China

Contents

MINDFULNESS IN ACTION

PREPARING FOR CHANGE

LEARNING TO MEDITATE

EXPANDING INTO MINDFULNESS

YOUR NEW MINDFUL LIFE

"Mindfulness is
the awareness that
arises in the moment,
nonjudgmentally."

JON KABAT-ZINN

1
WHERE TO BEGIN

With its roots deep in ancient cultures, and with a strong affinity to Buddhist practice, mindfulness has proved its benefits to us over many centuries. But in the last fifty years or so, it has gained new champions who have picked up and developed the concept in a secular, rather than purely religious, way for our modern generations.

What is mindfulness?

You may already know something about mindfulness, or perhaps you've just heard about its many benefits. This is because research into the subject has yielded powerful results with regard to its effectiveness in giving us a better experience of life. It has been used to control pain, cope with mental-health issues, and even alleviate the effects of chronic illnesses. Besides all this, practitioners report that it has enhanced their overall feeling of well-being, irrespective of whether they have a specific reason for practicing mindfulness.

However, it seems far more difficult to explain exactly what we mean by the word. Mindfulness is a state of mind in which we focus our awareness on whatever we are doing at that moment. It may be cooking or reading, cleaning or working, or simply sitting watching the birds and enjoying a cup of tea. The unifying element is that all our attention is directed at what we are doing, without thinking about the hundred other things we think we should or could be doing. It is allowing the thoughts

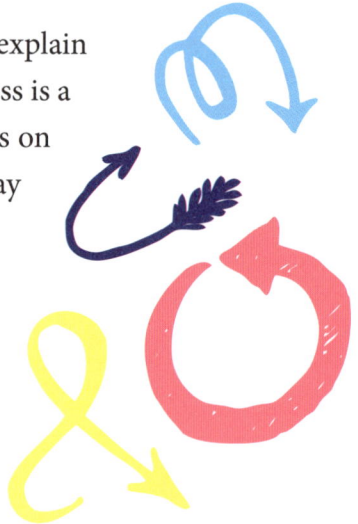

that naturally arise in the mind to pass you by without following them and taking your attention elsewhere.

Part of becoming more mindful is not dwelling on the past or looking too much into the future. If we look backwards too frequently, we often make the mistake of turning over events in our minds and reshaping them in various ways, wishing they could have had a better outcome. Or we play out how we would like things to happen, even though we know that the scenario we are inventing is unlikely. We cannot change the past; it is done. Of course, we can change the future, but the surest foundation for a brighter future lies in how we deal with the present.

By embracing mindfulness and trying to live in as mindful a way as we can, we can experience so much more of the beauty of the world because we view it afresh every moment. It takes us away from judgment or recrimination and simply sees things as they are. This can help us achieve a contented and calm mind, give us confidence in our self-worth and present us with a healthier, happier outlook on life.

ELEMENTS OF MINDFULNESS

The importance of not casting judgment on either ourselves or others is part of being mindful. Once we introduce emotional elements and start to make judgments, we stop being objective, and our emotions can unbalance our observations.

With mindfulness, our rational thoughts and feelings are in perfect balance, granting us an invaluable perspective on life that can help us be the best person we can be because we:

- are able to be fully aware in the moment and appreciate the present in all its detail

- meditate regularly to find inner calm to influence our view of life

- acknowledge and respect emotions and understand how individual emotions make us feel

- are able to release emotions so that they do not control us

- value silence as a positive, not just an absence of sound

- respond thoughtfully, not automatically

- don't dwell nostalgically on the past

- don't think constantly about what is coming next

Above all, to be mindful is to find contentment in each moment.

Meditation

When we aim to bring mindfulness into our lives, the ultimate achievement is to be mindful at all times. That is not easy, nor is it achieved by most people, but it is a goal toward which we can all aim—while not attaching ourselves unduly to it.

The route most people take to help them toward mindfulness is to learn to meditate. Meditating is a way of stilling your thoughts so that you remove yourself from the everyday, finding a place of complete calm and serenity. Again, this can take a little practice, but that in itself is of value, and there is no pressure to move at a particular speed or to find a level of relaxation and calm that is deeper than anyone else's. This is your journey; take it at your own pace and let your intuition guide you.

When you reach that place of inner calm, you can simply relax into that serene space and use the meditation to slow down your brain waves so you feel completely relaxed.

With further practice, meditation can be a place where you take experiences that you need to process. From that calm and objective standpoint, difficult circumstances can be reviewed. You will be able to begin to observe your experiences of the world around you and, in particular, how your emotions influence the way you perceive those experiences and how you react to them. It may be, perhaps, that you reacted harshly to a curt email from a colleague, interpreting her brevity as discourteous; but when you review the situation objectively and take away your anger, you can see that, actually, she was probably just tired and desperate to get home after a long day at work.

While you are in that calm place, you can try looking for the positive, for the beautiful, for the fair and honest. Looking at things as they are without attaching interpretations to them will change their ability to have control of you. If you take negative emotion out of the equation, events no longer have the potential to cause you the stress they once did. However, it is also possible to mindfully and nonjudgmentally accept negative emotions by sitting with them until they pass. Either way, if you can change the way you look at experiences, you can change how they affect you and the ultimate outcome.

Becoming mindful is the result of applying the focus of meditation to the everyday, giving you a more relaxed view to guide you smoothly through the day's activities and stresses.

The origins of mindfulness

It is impossible to say where the original roots of mindfulness actually lie, but it has definitely been practiced since ancient times, almost certainly longer. Ancient Greek philosophers—such as Aristippus, Thales and Epictetus—expounded the notion that happiness was central to existence, and that we should try to find happiness by making the most of each circumstance as it came along. By paying full attention to life as it passed before us, we would be able to enjoy it to the full, and that way would lead to contentment.

The Greeks were also aware of the importance of our perception in our notions of reality. Epictetus wrote: "What concerns us is not the way things actually are, but rather the way we think things are." In other words, a situation might be quite innocuous, but because we are viewing it from a standpoint colored by emotion—be that anger, love, jealousy or whatever—our interpretation is different. For example, if you are in a secure relationship and your partner compliments an attractive woman, you will probably agree and acknowledge that it's perfectly normal for him to find her appealing. On the other hand, if your relationship is not as solid, you might feel threatened by his comments and think it possible that he might even decide to act on them. The comment is essentially the same, but the interpretations of it are quite different.

Positivity and self-belief were also much valued by the ancients, not least the somewhat aggressive Romans, whose empire, at its height, spread across Europe. They believed wholeheartedly—and somewhat literally—in seizing the moment. The surviving writings of one Roman Emperor, Marcus Aurelius, reveal him as an advocate of maintaining a positive attitude and not allowing negative thoughts to take hold and control your personality.

Confucian thought developed along similar lines, with the notion of the power to change our circumstances by changing our attitude toward them. The Confucians defined eight steps to self-cultivation and social harmony; the third step dealt with the mind. That step involved searching for an awareness very similar to how we understand mindfulness, a state in which a person begins to really listen, not just to hear.

Buddhist understanding

Mindfulness is at the heart of Buddhist philosophy, and is one of the eight principles that the Buddha embraced and promoted for everyone to follow. These eight principles are grouped into three areas:

WISDOM

Understanding

Intention

CONDUCT

Speech

Action

Livelihood

MEDITATION

Effort

Mindfulness

Concentration

Following a Buddhist path means putting all these skills into practice with the intention of achieving the ultimate aim: finding happiness.

Achieving this was to practice mindfulness, the state of being in the moment and really relishing the potential of every moment. For the Buddhists, as for others, the route to this was through using meditation to change thought processes and, by doing so, change an individual's perception of the world around them. The Buddha believed totally in the concept that we can change our circumstances by changing our thoughts and our attitude. To be able to do that, we need to cultivate awareness of our body and mind.

The same principles apply to many different philosophies, both ancient and modern.

The development of mindfulness

In the religious sphere, mindfulness also includes the element of prayer, as clearly the focus of a religious meditation is an understanding of oneself in relation to God. The uniqueness of Christian meditation, for example, is that you are meditating on God and your relationship to him through Jesus.

Alongside the religious views that were prominent in the past, mindfulness has now been embraced in both religious and secular thinking; in fact, it is open to everyone of any faith (or none), and welcomes an individualistic approach to the common goal of achieving contentment.

We are now in a position in which we hold a simple tool that can help make our lives better, more fulfilling and rewarding from every perspective. By cultivating awareness of ourselves in the present moment, we can gain understanding, confidence and an attitude that will help us smooth our daily path through life. This, in turn, will help us be the happy and contented people we want to be.

"What is this life if,
full of care,
We have no time
to stand and stare?"

WILLIAM HENRY DAVIES

2

MODERN LIFE

Modern life is lived at frantic pace, and we are so busy looking ahead—thinking about all those other things we could and should be doing—that we constantly stumble over our own feet. How often do you see two people walking side by side on the sidewalk, heads bowed, concentrating on their phones, each in a world of their own, removed from where they are and what they are doing?

Too much, too fast, too random

It may be a cliché to say that life was simpler years ago, but it is true that while technology has brought immense advantages, it has also created problems that have not been encountered before.

The development of technology has taken over many time-consuming jobs, and therefore freed us from many of life's mundane tasks. In theory, this should give us more time to socialize and relax—but empirical evidence suggests this is far from the case.

In fact, technology has opened up so many new possibilities, and brought so many more things within our reach, that it has had the opposite effect. You don't have to trawl your memory to recall the guy who starred in the film you saw last week—you Google it. In fact, the verb "to Google" has been in the *Oxford English Dictionary*—the most widely recognized source in the world—since 2006. You can do almost anything on

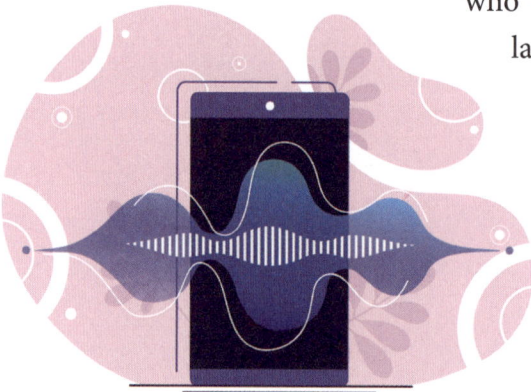

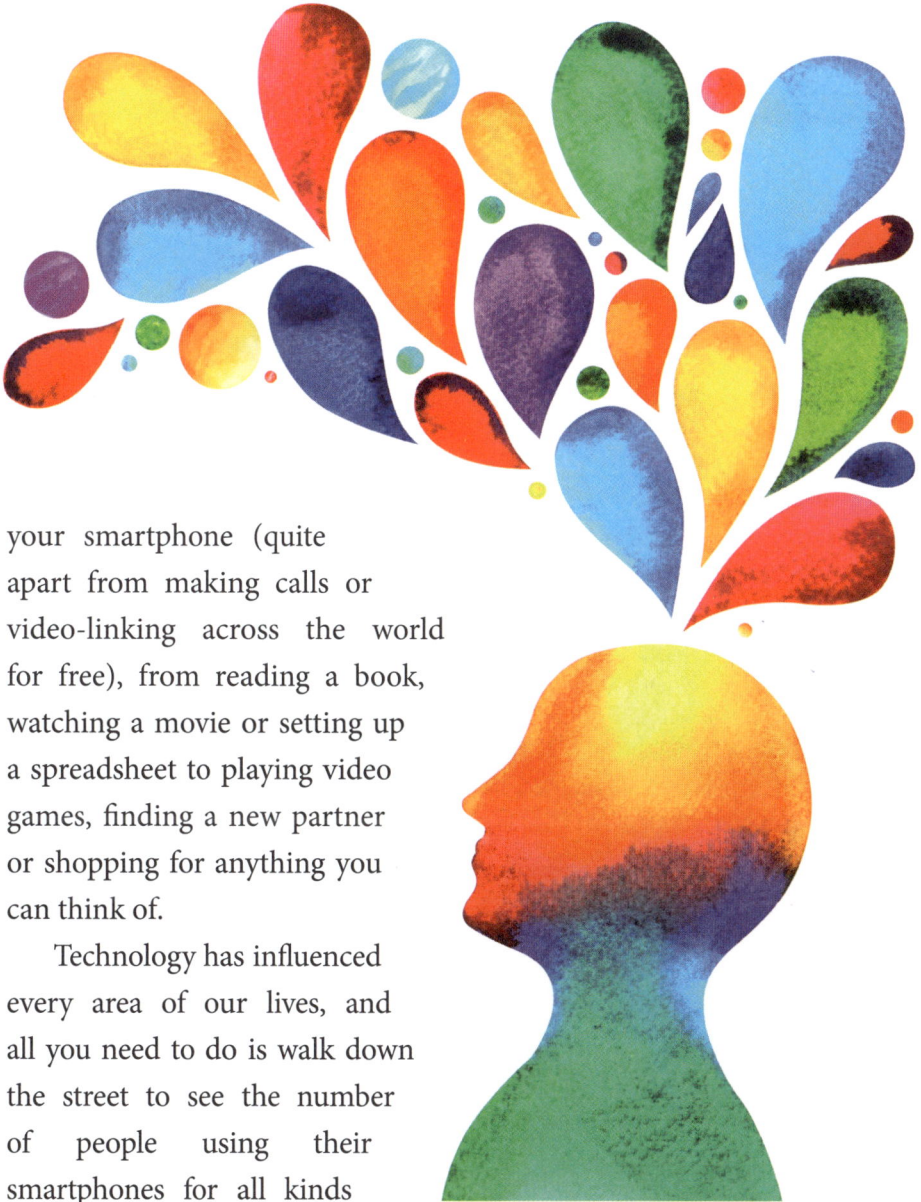

your smartphone (quite apart from making calls or video-linking across the world for free), from reading a book, watching a movie or setting up a spreadsheet to playing video games, finding a new partner or shopping for anything you can think of.

Technology has influenced every area of our lives, and all you need to do is walk down the street to see the number of people using their smartphones for all kinds of things—conversations, following maps, paying for goods, texting, listening to music—and to realize how ubiquitous they have become.

FAST AND FURIOUS

In addition, the speed at which information can be delivered has made us impatient to have instant solutions. Everything is immediate. Items at the top of the pile are dealt with first, regardless of any other priority, so if you miss your chance for consideration, then you may languish at the bottom, and simply be forgotten.

So, as we begin to run down the hill, our speed increases exponentially as we go down, breaking into a trot, then a run, until we are all traveling

at such a pace, fending off information we don't need, dealing with what we do, all the while trying to match the social whirl that is hurtling alongside us.

GREAT EXPECTATIONS

At work, at home, with family, friends or colleagues, the pressures on our lives come thick and fast. Pressure to have everything in the latest model, whether you need the subtleties of what it can do or not. Pressure for achievement. Pressure to be first to embrace change. Pressure for speed. Pressure to find time to try the latest exercise craze, the hippest celebrity diet, or the newest health issue they've found a name for. From every direction, these demands are bombarding us. It can sometimes seem impossible to achieve a balance, to tell what actually is important from what is not. While trying to find solutions, this can lead to overthinking, confusion and inaction—none of which actually gets you anywhere. It is also all very time-consuming, leaving you even less time to find space for relaxation.

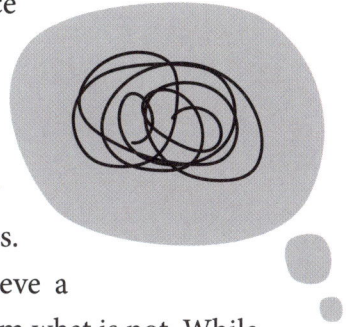

SOCIAL MEDIA

We could hardly escape talking here about social media, around which so many people's lives revolve. There are advantages, of course: it is a huge benefit to keep in touch via text, phone or video with friends across the world at any distance or in any time zone.

But it is worth reminding ourselves from time to time that someone's internet presence—on whatever platform—is only what they choose to share about themselves. If they have spent a wonderful day on an outing with friends, then they are likely to broadcast it. But a day spent cleaning the house, working or feeling low are less likely to hit their personal headlines. So the impression you get can be that, while your life is one of ups and downs and plenty of boring parts, theirs is just one long party. Then, sadly, there are those who simply do not tell the truth, but choose to adopt a social-media persona.

If we are mindful of all these factors, then we can use the best aspects of technology and social media to our advantage, sharing our lives meaningfully with those who are close to us. For those who need more strength and guidance in order not to be adversely influenced by such manipulations of the truth, using a mindful approach to modern technology will certainly help. Some use social-media "fasts" to try to regain their peace of mind. However, surprisingly, the mindful

approach does not necessarily require us to pull the plug on social media entirely. It is more to be watchful of how we use it, what we are feeling when we use it, and how we react to those feelings.

If you find yourself checking your social-media channels reflexively, try instead to bring yourself into awareness of what you're doing and what you're feeling as you scan your feeds. Is your mood affected by pictures of friends having a good time, perhaps at a function to which you weren't invited? Does it make you feel sad, lonely, upset? Conversely, are you uplifted and amused by humorous stories and films of cute animals? Become aware of the feelings—good or bad—and see where they sit in your body. Then try bringing your awareness to that place—be it your throat that is constricted due to anger, or your belly that is softened by laughter. Stay in the moment and turn away from your social-media feed when you are ready.

Then repeat this exercise every time you check your feed. Decide over time if the feelings that arise are ones you wish to sit with, or if you can do without them. Adjust your use of the medium accordingly.

What is our multi-tech life doing to us?

It is a fact that if you put too much pressure on anything, it may bend, but eventually it will break. If we continue to put ourselves under pressure through unrealistic lifestyles and expectations, at first we can adapt. But eventually the pressure will increase, and we will start functioning at below-optimum levels. In extreme cases, we'll contract physical or mental problems, and we'll break.

We all know our own physical "Achilles' heel"—our weakest point. When we are overstressed or about to succumb to a virus, some people get a sore throat, some a headache; for others, the first sign of illness is an upset stomach. The body gives way at its weakest point. So whether it manifests as exhaustion, sleeplessness, backaches, headaches or IBS, many physical issues can be instigated—or at least exacerbated—by tension and over-stress.

OVER-STRESS

I use the words "over-stress" because I think "stress" is grossly overused and has been stripped of its meaning. Stress, in itself, is not a problem—it is simply part of the physics of life. A bridge is built specifically to cope with the stresses that will be placed upon it as a result of it doing its job, and a human is programmed to cope with a certain degree of stress as a result of living and working in society. That stress can be a positive motivator. It can provides the incentive to finish an important report, get to your child's school play on time, learn a new skill or study hard for a test.

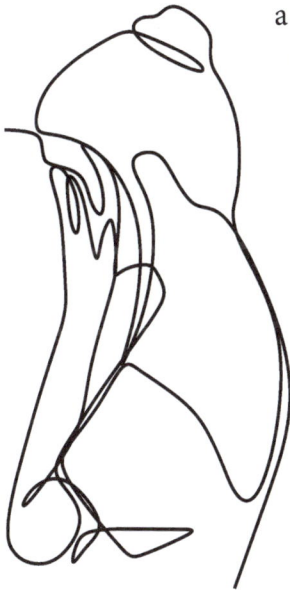

Only when the pressure is relentless and impossible to resolve does it become a negative issue, which is the situation when you are over-stressed. When this happens, the negative effects can be physical or mental, and will be different for each person.

LIVING IN THE PAST

Trying to cope with modern life by looking for a successful pattern of behavior you have used before is often not successful, largely because if you look back and repeat what you've done before, the outcome is likely to be the same—and this means you are setting yourself up to repeat the same mistakes. That will sap your precious energy but not necessarily take you forward, to where you want to be.

Living in the present—being mindful—on the other hand, leaves behind mistakes of the past and allows you to make your decisions on the information available to you without baggage holding you back. Loosening those bonds is a great release of tension. You use your past experiences, of course, because they are part of what makes you who you are. But you do so from a new, clearer perspective.

I'M DOWN

The same is true of psychological issues, from having more than your fair share of down days to more serious cases of mental-health breakdown. If

our minds are over-stressed, this can result in all kinds of mental-health issues, most commonly anxiety and depression.

It may be that a particular event or series of events have triggered a problem, or perhaps an accumulation of small incidents has eroded your confidence and sent you into what feels like a downward spiral. Perhaps you are simply feeling overwhelmed, with too much to do and too many expectations, cramming your life with meaningless detail that doesn't have any real relevance. The spiral becomes tighter, and can leave you feeling out of control and not knowing where to turn.

At such times, professional help is vital—and the sooner the better. Asking for help is not an easy thing to do in any circumstances, but if you are able to take a step toward getting it, you will be rewarded. For less severe descents into feelings of chaos, mindfulness training can help you process any negative emotions you may be harboring and leave you more able to let go of the past and stop projecting past mistakes onto future opportunities. There is no suggestion that this will be quick or easy, but breaking the vicious cycle could be the best start you can make.

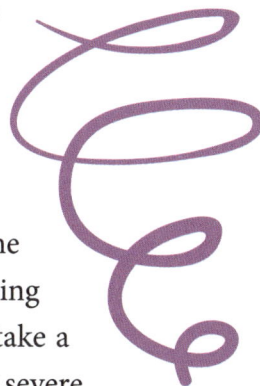

SLEEPLESS WHEREVER YOU ARE

Especially if you are feeling tense, you may find it difficult to sleep or to get an uninterrupted night's sleep. Mindfulness should bring you a greater sense of calm, and an ability to relax that should help you stop the wheels of your mind from turning and allow you to drift naturally into uninterrupted sleep.

Using meditation on its own as a method of relaxation can be useful. You may want to do the muscle relaxation exercise (see page 86) as you are lying in bed, and this should help you drift off into a relaxed sleep.

As you continue with your meditation and your mind clears, switching off completely should become easier, and your more relaxed brain patterns should enable you to sleep through the night.

Mindfulness in the modern world

If we pull all these elements together, we'll get a pretty good picture of what mindfulness is and is not, and what it could mean to us in the 21st century.

Mindfulness is:

- an attitude of mind in which you focus your full attention on the immediate moment

- a choice that impacts every aspect of our lives

- completely open to those of any faith, or none

- a positive force for change

- totally non-judgmental

- a lifestyle choice that uses meditation as its key

- not nostalgic or intent on dwelling in the past

- not projecting into the future

- an ability to observe and listen, not just hear

ADVANTAGES

Each of these characteristics of mindfulness can have positive implications for us if we embrace the practice of stilling the mind in regular meditation.

Personal advantages include:

- cultivating an ability to enjoy your life moment by moment

- finding a greater understanding of your emotions and how they affect your view of yourself and those around you

- learning how to respect your strengths and understand your weaknesses

- being able to forgive yourself for mistakes

- being able to forgive others

- a calmness that brings increased self-confidence

- physical and mental well-being

- the ability to be objective and non-judgmental, and to assess situations without irrelevant or unhelpful emotions

- contentment

Social advantages include:

- being able to observe and experience without judgment, which cements relationships

- positive attitudes that can be shared across secular and religious communities to have a uniquely good effect

- being a good listener, and acting on the insights that can bring, is a valuable ability that has the potential to improve both personal and professional relationships

"This work strongly supports the hypothesis that meditation can change the structure and function of the brain, and that these changes are associated with cognitive and emotional benefits. While there is still much to understand, research findings generally support the use of meditation as a powerful technique in clinical practice."

MICHAEL TREADWAY AND SARA LAZAR

3

BUT CAN YOU PROVE IT?

The brain is a hugely complex organ, and we have barely scratched the surface in terms of understanding how it works and its potential. But scientists have an extensive knowledge that is increasing all the time, and their research continues to confirm that over-stress is bad for us, while mindfulness is good.

What happens when we meditate?

For centuries, the benefits of meditation and mindfulness have been experienced by people across the globe. Now we are beginning to improve our knowledge of how the brain works, and scientists have been looking to prove that meditation actually does affect the brain, and they want to discover how it happens.

Scientific studies have to be rigorous, and clearly define the comparative tests they are undertaking and the control by which they are judged. By its nature, mindfulness is not easy to test. But brain-wave patterns when meditating can be measured and mapped to compare with measurements taken when not meditating. Modern, sophisticated scanning techniques can detect electrical activity in the brain, and calculate variations in this activity, the strength or weakness of the parts of the brain involved, and their relationship to each other. Such changes all affect our mood and behavior, and they are all positively affected by meditation.

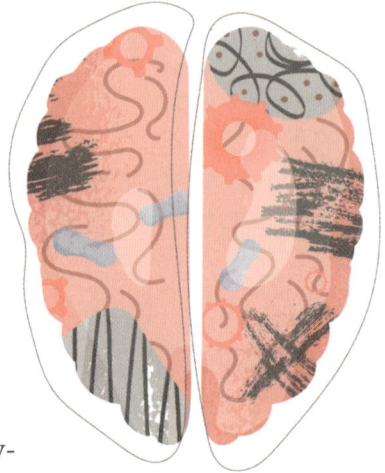

THE PARTS OF THE BRAIN INVOLVED IN MINDFULNESS PRACTICE

In very simple terms, certain parts of the brain process our thoughts and emotions.

- **Rational**: The lateral prefrontal cortex is the sensible, rational part that looks at things from a logical viewpoint.

- **Personal**: The medial prefrontal cortex relates experiences to what has happened to you in the past, separating people you view as being like you and those you don't. This is the home of empathy.

- **Bodily**: The insula monitors bodily sensations and measures the strength of the response.

- **Emotional**: The amygdala controls the emotional response, notably fear, and shrinks when there is less stress.

- **Memory**: The hippocampus stores memory.

- **Decision-making**: This function is performed by the ingulate cortex.

A LITTLE ABOUT BRAIN WAVES

There is always some electrical activity in the brain in the form of rhythmic fluctuations of voltage between parts of the brain that result in a flow of electric current that we call brain waves. The frequency of the pulse determines the type of brain wave.

- beta waves pulse at 14-30Hz when we are awake, alert and focused

- alpha waves pulse at 8-14Hz when we are relaxed but alert

- theta waves pulse at 4-8Hz when we are drowsy

- delta waves pulse at 0.5-4Hz when we are deeply asleep

WHEN WE MEDITATE

When we meditate, our brains move between moments of pure concentration and moments of distraction, when random, everyday thoughts pop into our heads. The more practiced you are, the less that will happen, and the sooner you will be able to dismiss those interruptions.

Nonetheless, you can expect meditation to be a fluctuating state. Having said that, meditation, at whatever level, can change the way the brain is working and the relationships between parts of the brain. This ability to change—neuroplasticity—has far-reaching implications. It means we can use meditation to influence our brain-wave patterns to encourage focus, emotional control and thoughtful decision-making. Of course, it also suggests that if regular behavior can make such changes, if we stop those behaviors, then the brain waves can revert, so meditation, for example, needs to be regular and ongoing.

Research results

Various scientific studies have sought to confirm the empirical evidence of the benefits of meditation. A Norwegian study compared the brain waves of experienced meditators when they were meditating to their brain waves when they were simply resting.

- The lack of delta waves during meditation and rest proved that sleep has a different impact on the brain than resting or meditation.

- Alpha waves associated with relaxed attention were strongest when subjects were meditating.

- Theta waves were strongest during rest.

The study proved that sleep, rest and meditation have three quite distinct effects on the brain, with the benefits of alpha waves being the most marked. People suffering from depression or anxiety tend to have more activity on the right side of the brain, rather than the norm, which shows more activity on the left side. However, studies have shown that those who meditate have further increased activity on the left side, suggesting that meditation has potential to both enhance mood and lift depression.

In studies at Massachusetts General Hospital, subjects were asked to meditate for 30 minutes a day; the changes in the strength and connectivity between the various parts of the brain were measured to see whether the brain could change in response to meditation. Within as few as eight weeks, subjects demonstrated a number of changes. The link between the amygdala and the prefrontal cortex was reduced, making it less likely that an overly emotional response would override a rational one, and improving mental capacity. Meditation also strengthened the medulla oblongata, which resulted in the subjects being less affected by negative emotions. There was also an improvement in the experience of depression and anxiety.

Other studies have indicated that those who meditated showed a heightened response to negative images of accidents, but brain patterns returned to normal more quickly, showing an improved ability to deal with emotions, coupled with the ability to let them go.

The seat of memory, the hippocampus, becomes more dense in practitioners of meditation, strengthening understanding. At the same time, there is a decrease in the density of the amygdala, the source of fear and over-stress.

Early studies have also suggested that meditation improves the brain's ability to protect itself against age-related cognitive decline, opening up the potential that we could learn how to head off, or eventually even control, the onset of memory loss, dementia or Alzheimer's—all conditions that cause anxiety and misery for sufferers and their families.

Many studies have confirmed that not only does the brain behave in a different way during meditation, but regular meditation over a prolonged period has an ongoing positive effect.

All of this evidence demonstrates that meditation, practiced for at least 10 minutes every day, really is worthwhile for health and well-being because of the way it affects the brain. If you then imagine that you can introduce mindfulness to the remaining waking hours of the day, you should increase those benefits considerably.

"No one cares
how much you know,
until they know
how much you care."

THEODORE ROOSEVELT (1858-1919)

4
MINDFULNESS IN ACTION

The aim of mindfulness is to teach you to appreciate each moment to its fullest. It should help you deal with emotions, allowing them to be expressed without taking over, restore your balance, help you feel comfortable with who you are—physically and mentally—and encourage you to value and care for yourself just as you do other people, basing healthy relationships on mutual respect.

Changing our attitude to what we can't control

We can't change everything in life so that the outcome is always good; we all know that many things are outside our control. But the sooner we can come to grips with how we approach the things that are outside our control, the easier life can be. Most of us have, at one time or another, had to work with someone we find intensely annoying— the reasons don't really matter, and the feelings are probably mutual. It's just a clash of personalities, a pairing that doesn't fit. Neither person can change the other, so there are two options: continue to allow yourself to feel aggravated and frustrated on a daily basis, or try to take the mindful approach to the relationship.

Those who embrace mindfulness will be able to meditate on the emotions they feel, acknowledge what they feel, and put them aside. They will think about the circumstances in which they have to interact, and accept that they will not be ideal, but will no longer be burdened by the backstory of things that have already happened or the projection of a future constantly having to relate to this person. In the moment, the situation becomes workable, more relaxed and far more conducive to further improvement.

Achieving this state of mindfulness may not happen overnight, but a regular, small commitment to meditation for at least 10 minutes a day should yield a great deal of progress within as little as eight weeks. Benefits can be physical or mental, but they all start with the brain and, through meditation, you optimize its function so that each element is in balance and working harmoniously.

Controlling pain

Physical pain is controlled in the brain, which communicates through the central nervous system to the areas of localized pain. As well as pain caused by damage of some kind to the tissues of the body—sprains, bruises, cuts, breaks—it is possible for tension and over-stress to be the cause of physical pain. It can also be the case that pain is experienced in a different part of the body from where it originates. An uneven gait, bad working posture or severe tension can result in back, neck or headaches, for example.

The mindful approach is to calm the brain waves through meditation, which can help ease the pain. It also encompasses our attitude to the pain in that it will encourage focus on the moment, rather than on the ongoing nature of the pain. This enhances the brain-wave patterns that strengthen positive thoughts and distract from the pain itself. In the case of tension headaches and other pain created by over-stress, meditation should help to relieve tension in the body and therefore take away the cause of the pain.

In addition, of course, you should be under the care of an appropriate medical adviser, and many people find guided exercises useful.

Coping with a chronic condition

Chronic conditions include such disorders as Parkinson's disease, muscular dystrophy, arthritis and multiple sclerosis. And, as we live longer and medical treatments continue to advance, an increasing number of people will be living with such conditions. For the most part, patients will receive specialized care and medication. But tension, mood, attitude and other factors have a considerable effect on many such conditions, so there is a lot that sufferers can do to help them manage their condition more successfully.

A chronic condition, by definition, involves a range of symptoms, the combination being unique to the individual. Some people experience mild symptoms that can be controlled with medication, while others have sporadic or intermittent symptoms, and some are seriously disabled. They may experience chronic pain, movement issues, cognitive problems and any number of other symptoms; plus, they may have to cope with side effects from their medication.

Underlying tension will always exacerbate certain symptoms, as will holding on to frustration, anger and feelings of helplessness, unfairness, loneliness or anger. If you are able to meditate regularly and extend the benefits into your everyday behavior, making it more mindful, it can help reduce that tension, which, in turn, can actually alleviate symptoms as well as promote a positive and constructive outlook.

General mood plays a huge part in many of these conditions, and if patients can maintain a positive frame of mind, they may notice that their symptoms have less impact, or are less erratic. Over-stress, tension and low mood all have the opposite effect. So it makes sense that the slowing of brain waves and the calming of the mind that occurs during meditation reduces the perception of discomfort, pain or other symptoms and enables those affected to live a more normal life, closer to their full potential.

Coping with mental health issues

"Although the world is full of suffering, it is full also of the overcoming of it."
Helen Keller

There was a time when people didn't talk about subjects such as depression and anxiety. They were considered taboo, and sufferers did so in silence, thinking that what they needed to do was "pull themselves together and deal with it," which is the advice many were given if they sought help.

Now we realize that mental health is just as important as physical health, and there are many treatments and therapies that can be advantageous. High-profile people are also beginning to talk more openly about their experiences, making it more acceptable to admit that you have suffered, or are suffering, from depression or other mental-health problems.

If you are a sufferer, then it's always advisable to get professional help at the earliest opportunity. There are many therapies that have proved successful, and the earlier the problem is tackled, the more likely it is that there will be a speedier and more successful outcome.

There are huge variations in the severity of such problems as depression and anxiety, and no one should underestimate their impact at any level. At best, they can make someone miserable; at worst, they can destroy lives. But if you are suffering from such problems, there is a lot you can do at the former end of the scale to lift the clouds that seem to hang over you. You can stop the vicious cycle of going over the same ground, which will enable you to stop blaming yourself or others for your problems.

Meditation is unlikely to offer immediate relief, but it should gradually help you find a place of calm and relaxation that you can resort to regularly. Over time, you will hopefully learn to find this place of peace when you need it, and it can become part of your everyday life.

Recognizing the emotions you feel is also important; identify what they are and how they make you feel, then find the strength to cast them aside. Try one at a time, so you don't bite off more than you can chew. As you work through each one, it should help you identify the source of your issues and, in doing so, you will feel you are beginning to regain control. Mindfulness will help you put tension and depression into perspective by allowing you to take a step back from the intensity of the emotions surrounding them. This provides a firm foundation for you to begin to identify the original sources of your problems, and take action to change the circumstances.

Dealing with uncomfortable feelings

A guest meditation by Leo Babauta

Leo Babauta is an author who writes on mindfulness and taking a more mindful approach to life. Here is his method to practice if you're feeling stressed, frustrated, lonely, sad or tired:

1 Notice that you're feeling this difficult emotion, and notice how it feels in your body. Bring a sense of curiosity to the sensations, just being present with them for a moment.

2 Notice what thoughts you have in your head that are causing the emotion. For example, you might be thinking, "They shouldn't treat me like that" or "Why does my job have to be so hard?" or "These people are stressing me out! Things should be more settled and

orderly," or other thoughts in that vein. Just notice whatever they are. Maybe write them down.

3 Notice that the thoughts are causing your difficulty. Not the situation — the thoughts. You might not believe that at first, but see if you can investigate whether that's true.

4 Ask yourself, "What would it be like if I didn't have these thoughts right now? What would my experience be right now?" The simple answer is that you're just having an experience — you have feelings in your body, but you also are experiencing a moment that has light, colors, sound, touch sensation on your skin, and so on. It's just an experience, a moment in time, not good or bad.

5 In fact, while this experience is neither good or bad, you can start to appreciate it for what it is, without the thoughts. Just seeing it as a fresh experience, maybe even appreciating the beauty of the moment. Maybe even loving the moment just as it is.

Obviously, some of this might take practice. But it's worth it, because while you might not be able to get rid of fatigue (some rest would help there), you can let go of the thoughts about fatigue that are causing you to be unhappy. You might not be able to get rid of loneliness, but you can let go of the downward spiral of thoughts and emotions that make the situation worse.

If you'd like to read more of Leo Babauta's work on mindfulness, visit zenhabits.net.

Anger management

"Anyone can be angry—that is easy. But to be angry with the right person, to the right degree, at the right time, for the right purpose and in the right way—that is not easy."

Aristotle

Anger that gets out of control or is inappropriate is rarely a solution to a problem, and usually only leads to an escalation of a difficult situation. If you can learn to step back from the situation that has made you lose your temper, and defuse the excess of emotion, then you should be able to handle situations more productively.

Because anger is such a strong emotion, it is best to take things slowly. When you're meditating, bring the situation that has provoked your anger into your mind and try to distance yourself from it. If you feel the anger rising, breathe deeply and slowly five times, then go back to try to face it again. Use visualization (see page 145) to imagine yourself coping in a calm and rational way with the difficulties you are facing.

For some people, anger is associated with guilt, because as children they were taught that anger was a "bad" emotion that should be suppressed. Consider this during meditation if this is the case for you. If so, use your time of meditation to break that connection. We are all entitled to be angry at times. The important thing is to recognize it, deal with the cause and not let it fester.

Steer clear of trying to blame anyone—including yourself—for your anger. It is no one's fault, and trying to allocate blame will only send you into a vicious circle that will feed your anger because you will not find a solution. The best way forward is to break the cycle.

CONTROLLING FEAR

Fear is another strong emotion that can grip you and make you feel powerless. But such emotions only exist in the mind, and can be conquered if, as Dale Carnegie famously said, "you will only make up your mind to do so." He went on to remind us that fear does not exist anywhere but in the mind.

The relaxed and calm state of meditation will allow you to practice examining your fear in a nonconfrontational and nonthreatening way, taking the power away from the object of your fear and restoring it to you. You could even try visualization, using an object to represent what you are afraid of.

DESTRUCTIVE AND ADDICTIVE BEHAVIOR

Anger is the most common form of destructive behavior, but addictive behavior is similarly, if not more, injurious. It can often be the result of a lack of self-worth.

No doubt you will also find areas of your character that are less strong, as we all do—one person is creative, another good at sports, a third mathematically inclined. They are facts, not judgments. Look at your so-called weaknesses and acknowledge them. You may want to work to improve them, or you may be quite happy not to; we all have our perfections and imperfections. As an exercise, try looking at the lives of a few well-known people who have wonderful talents combined with serious difficulties. Even those we look up to are only human.

Enjoying the moment

Mindfulness teaches us that to enjoy our lives, we must learn to observe and enjoy what is in front of us right now. So often, we are thinking about something else and distracted by thoughts of what has happened in the past or what may happen in the future. Focus on what you are currently experiencing— emotionally and physically— and you will find you get so much more out of every second.

PERSPECTIVE AND BALANCE

This mindfulness, which we can spread through our lives from its heart in our regular meditation, is designed to realign our perspective. It can help us look at everything without judgment—just assessing it as it is. If it's something we cannot change, the only thing we can alter is the way we look at it. If we continue to turn over the issue or incident, looking to attach blame or recrimination—gnawing at it like a dog with a bone— that will only make us more anxious. Increased anxiety leads to more concern and more anxiety, and that negative emotion can seep through our whole life.

What we are aiming for is learning to be more objective in our view so that we can look at the incident and acknowledge our part in it, what we did and how it made us feel. Having acknowledged that, learn to put aside the negative emotions and walk away from them.

WELL-BEING

General well-being is something we all strive for, even though it is one of the most difficult things to define. Essentially, it is a state in which you are physically and emotionally content with how your life is.

This is one of the primary goals of mindfulness. When you are able to appreciate each moment of your life as you experience it, you can make the best of each moment. Looking back will not be tangled with unresolved emotions; looking forward will be with a calm and realistic perspective. You will be looking to find the positive in everything, maintain the balance between the elements of your life, and reduce over-stress.

CREATIVITY

Being able to enjoy the moment often releases a streak of creativity of which you may not have been aware. This is because you are feeling more relaxed and able to look outward; and, perhaps, spending time trying to be more observant of things around you has been encouraging new areas of your brain to spark into action.

Feeding your confidence

Being mindful of the value of everything and being able to review, understand and acknowledge how different emotions make you feel puts you in control. During meditation sessions, finding self-knowledge should be a boost to confidence and to the ability to relate to other people. Confidence comes from knowing and accepting yourself—"warts and all"—and valuing yourself equally with those around you.

Establishing your own value is at the core of mindfulness. Starting with realistic expectations, work slowly to focus on understanding yourself and being balanced in your self-awareness.

Look at your strengths. Compare them with other people's strengths only if it helps you understand and value your own skills. This is not a competition; it's more of an appreciation. It doesn't help to brag about your skills, but don't denigrate them either. Don't say to yourself, "Anyone could do that!" It is probably not true. Even something you consider simple—like baking a cake or sewing on a button—may be beyond the scope of many people.

Confidence is also at the heart of doing better at work, and improving your social skills and self-awareness. It can enhance your leadership qualities, make you more decisive, and help you deal with conflict without getting overcome with emotion. It is about finding a fundamental respect for yourself and the many good qualities you possess while forgiving yourself for your weaknesses and not seeing them as the focus of other people's censure.

SOCIABILITY AND RELATIONSHIPS

Improving your confidence so that you value yourself equally with everyone else will help promote healthy relationships with your family, friends and colleagues; it gives you empathy and understanding of others, and at the same time acknowledges your own value. You can then take responsibility for your share of the relationship but not shoulder all of the burden.

Confidence will also help you go out and enjoy yourself more easily, because you know that you have something to offer, and are open and receptive to other people's ideas. You should enjoy your newfound energy and enthusiasm.

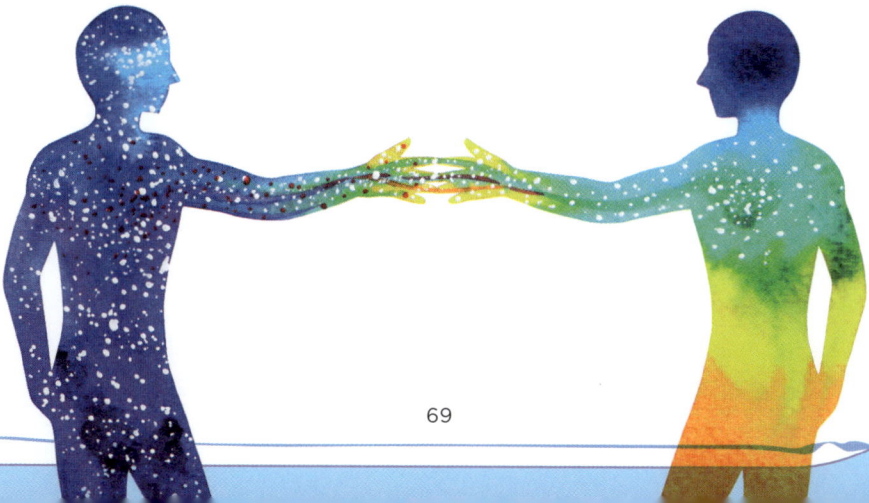

Alice:
"Would you tell me, please, which way I ought to go from here?"

Cheshire Cat: "That depends a good deal on where you want to get to."

LEWIS CARROLL

5

PREPARING FOR CHANGE

If you are embarking on any venture—especially a life-changing one—then you are advised to do some planning. The same is true for your quest for mindfulness. A good place to start is by looking at your current situation. Just as Google Maps needs to know your location and destination, you need to plan your route to mindfulness. Think about where you are and what you want to achieve by bringing mindfulness into your life. Then you can plan your meditation sessions to help you get there.

Making up your mind

Y ou're already thinking about working toward a state of mindfulness, but there are all kinds of variables. It will speed your progress if you think them through before you start.

It might help you create a framework for your mindfulness studies if you look at your current situation and think about the areas of your life and the priorities in them. You might divide your life into these areas:

HOME SOCIAL WORK OTHER

Then list the kinds of things you do under each heading, including how important they are and how much time you spend on them. Include traveling, sleeping, reading the paper, cooking and, if relevant at this stage, doing nothing. (If you never indulge in doing nothing, now is the time to learn.) This will start to give you an idea of whether your life is in balance and whether you're spending a good proportion of each day on the things that you have to do rather than the things you want to do. Clearly, there will be many of the former, and the proportions will fluctuate on a weekly basis, but it's all about striking that balance.

Assess your personality

It might also be interesting to make some notes on your personality, how you view the world and how you interact with other people.

- how would you describe yourself in a few words?

- what are your strengths?

- do you feel you have some weaknesses in your character?

- how do you behave in relationships with friends, family, colleagues or partners?

- do you make new friends easily?

- what do others say about you that you do not recognize?

- what do others expect of you, and you of them?

- are you cautious when meeting new people?

- do you have a strong self-image?

- how do you feel about your appearance? What do you like and dislike?

- how easily are you distracted?

- do you find it hard to concentrate?

- do you find silence rewarding or irksome?

Your answers will help you decide how to plan your meditation so it's rewarding for you in your quest for mindfulness.

It will be interesting to look at your answers again in three months, to see if things have changed.

The time factor

Think about how you're going to fit meditation into your routine, and what time is best for you. We've established that the regularity of your meditation sessions is important, so it's better to allocate a short length of time to start with, then build up gradually as you feel the benefits. Ten minutes a day is a good place to start, although if you are able to spend a little more time on it—say, 30 minutes—you should achieve quicker results. But it's better to do a little and do it regularly than "binge" meditate and then do nothing.

Are you a morning or an evening person? Can you find a gap before school or work in which you could meditate, and really set yourself up for the day? Maybe a lunch break is what you need to restore calm and focus? Is your bus or train home quiet and uncrowded enough that you could use the journey for meditation, to calm you and shed the frustrations of the day? (Once you become proficient, this won't matter so much, if at all.) Would it be better to meditate in the evening?

PERCEPTION OF TIME

If you think you can't even manage 10 minutes, let's put it into perspective. Just that small fraction of time devoted to meditation can have an impact on the rest of your day.

We shouldn't be distracted by the speed of modern life, by the fact that there's so much to do, and we are expected to do it all, and do it quickly. Slowing down allows us to savor each moment with more appreciation.

It's also a common complaint that time seems to speed up as you get older. And it's true. The numbers themselves are only important in their relationship to one another. Let's say that at the age of one, we have lived for 52 weeks, so in our experience of the passage of time, one week represents 1/52 of our total existence. By the time we're ten, that week becomes 1/520, so it seems to move more quickly. At 40, the ratio is 1/2,080, and by 60, it is 1/3,120, and so on.

So if time is both precious and speeding up, it must also be increasing in value and is not to be wasted. We owe it to ourselves to make the best of it. Unfortunately, if we want to add an activity to our schedule, a block of time will not simply open up in front of us. Look for a crack and make the time in your existing schedule, because it will have so much benefit.

STICK TO MODEST EXPECTATIONS

However hard you try, there simply aren't enough hours in the day to do it all. If you really can't find time for meditation every day, then perhaps every other day will be possible. Otherwise, another look at your schedule might be helpful to find something else that can be cut back to allow you some time for meditation. You may be able to discard some things, learn to delegate, or decide that you can spend less time in some areas to allow yourself more time in others.

Habits are harder to break than principles

Having decided that you are going to meditate for 10 minutes every day, the way to make sure you continue is to make it a habit. Rather than thinking you'll fit it in when you get a spare 10 minutes, plan it into your day.

Be firm with yourself, especially for the first week or two, and don't deviate from your plan. By that time, it should have started to become a habit that you will not want to break.

WHAT IS HOLDING YOU BACK?

With all this positivity, if you still don't take the plunge, try to list five things that are holding you back. You might find that they're the very things that demand attention when you start to meditate.

These things are holding me back:

1

2

3

4

5

This is how I'm going to deal with them:

1 _____

_____

2 _____

_____

3 _____

_____

4 _____

_____

5 _____

_____

"Mindfulness develops attention, concentration and the ability to simply be present with little or no future orientation, past orientation or goal orientation—choosing to be a human being rather than a human doing."

IAN GAWLER

6
LEARNING TO MEDITATE

It's easy to say you should meditate for 10 minutes in order to begin to bring mindfulness into your life, but where do you start? And how it is actually done? Here is simple step-by-step technique that you can use to begin your meditation. Once you have mastered the basics, then you can develop your technique through further study and experimentation.

Setting the scene

Although seasoned meditators can often take themselves out of the most difficult situations in order to restore their equanimity, beginners are not likely to achieve anything sitting uncomfortably in a noisy place. So the first thing to do is give some thought to what meditation is like, and how you're going to make it work for you, by setting the scene.

Find somewhere comfortable where you find it easy to relax, either sitting or lying down, whichever you prefer. Wear casual clothing and have the room at an optimum temperature. The keyword is comfortable.

TIMING

It doesn't matter what time of day you decide to meditate, but it should be when you will be uninterrupted for as long as you wish. You will not succeed if you are distracted by noise, or if you have to interrupt your thoughts to answer the phone or give instructions to children or someone else in the next room.

After you've been meditating for a while, you should find that you can take yourself out of any noisy or distracting situation—in fact, you can use your meditative skills to do just that—but it takes time and regular practice.

The feeling that you are trying to achieve is a completely relaxed state of mind—a gentle sense of awareness without engagement.

MUSIC OR SOUNDS

Whatever sounds you find relaxing and soothing, but that don't demand your attention, are suitable. However, only use sounds if you find silence intrusive. If you use music, it should be as a backdrop, not something that's clamoring for your attention. Some people use sounds like birdsong. Generally, it is best to avoid music with lyrics, because the words tend to be distracting.

FRAGRANCE

Similarly, some people find a fragrant candle or incense relaxing, while other don't. Start without, then try incense or a scented candle—which tend to be more subtle—with a fragrance of something like lavender or ylang ylang if you think it might help you relax.

Physical relaxation

Settle down in your comfortable place and begin to relax your muscles. An easy way to do this is to use the contrasting feeling of contracting them first so you know what that feels like, then relaxing them. Start with your head and face. Frown, screw up your face and squeeze it together, then release and feel the difference. Then go through your body, clenching each muscle group one at a time, holding for 5 seconds, then releasing.

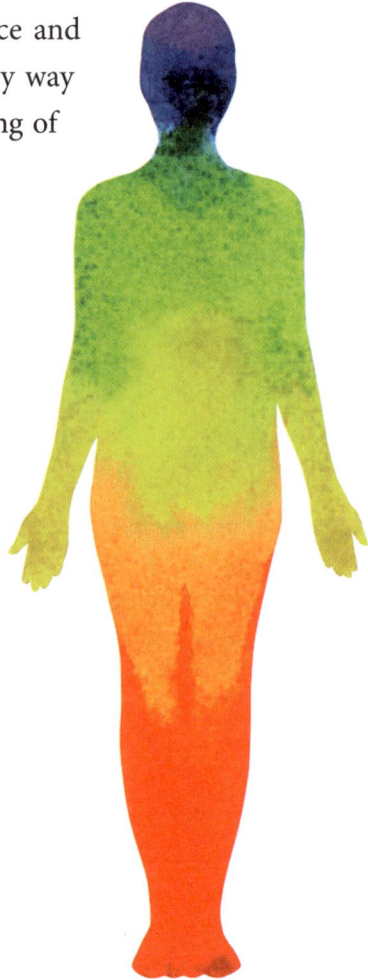

So, starting at the top:

- eyebrows

- face

- neck and shoulders

- arms

- hands

- pelvis

- thighs

- calves

- feet and toes

All the time, breathe in deeply and slowly, in and out through your nose.

As you become more experienced, you will find you are able to move through this exercise much more quickly, or even do away with it altogether and go straight to a physically relaxed state.

Moving into the moment

From physical relaxation, you can move to focusing on to how you are feeling emotionally. You may be thinking about that moment only, or looking at an incident that has been troubling you. Eliminate everything else from your mind. Focus with your full intensity so you begin to see details that you may have never noticed before.

- One at a time, think about the emotions you're feeling. Identify them. What are you feeling? Anger, sadness, frustration, anxiety? Think about how they make you feel. Accept that you are feeling that emotion; don't try to deny it. But don't blame yourself or anyone else for what you are feeling. Simply acknowledge that the emotion is there. Be observant of small details and be specific. Are you feeling it in a specific place in your body? Be aware of what it feels like and identify it: this is anger; this is sorrow; this is how it feels.

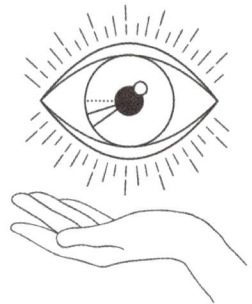

Perhaps you are thinking about a situation at work in which one of your ideas—delivered in confidence to your boss—has been successfully offered up in a meeting as his own idea. You may feel hot, your stomach tight; you may even feel like you want to strike out. Acknowledge that this is how anger or resentment makes you feel.

That process should help you distance yourself from the emotion. Once you can look at it dispassionately, without judgment, think about how it started and why you feel that way. What triggered it? What fueled it? What were the circumstances?

Now that you understand the emotion, let go of the need to control it. Discard it, let it go and move on. Watch it drifting away from you, powerless to hurt you. In the same way as you experienced the physical contrast between contraction and relaxation of your muscles. Feel how much lighter and calmer you are when you have dismissed the negative emotion.

You may need to address the same emotion or situation several times in order to fully deal with its impact. Work slowly and calmly, and with patience, and you will make progress.

CONCLUDING YOUR MEDITATION

Once you have let go of your emotion, relax for as long as you are comfortable, breathing deeply. Do not hurry to get back to your day. If thoughts of your to-do list come into your mind, observe them and then also let them drift away. Gradually let your awareness come back into the room until you are ready to move back into your normal consciousness. Hopefully, the calm induced by the meditation will help you feel more mindful throughout the day, now that you know the kind of feeling of detachment that you are aiming for in your everyday mental space.

Simple step-by-step meditation

Here is a simple sequence for you to follow and develop to make your own unique meditation program.

Setting the scene

◊ Find a place where you can sit or lie down comfortably at a mid-range, ambient temperature.

◊ Try to be somewhere where you will be quiet and not be interrupted.

◊ Put on relaxing music or introduce fragrance, if you wish.

Breathe

◊ Sit or lie still for a moment and breathe deeply so you begin to feel calm and relaxed.

◊ Breathe deeply—breathe in through your nose for a count of five, then out through your nose for a count of five. Inhale as deeply as you can, then expel as much air as you can. Maintain that rhythmic breathing throughout.

Muscle relaxation

◊ Now start to think about your muscle groups and, starting with your head, clench each group of muscles tightly, hold for a count of five, then release.

* Frown and screw up your face, hold, then release.

* Clench your neck and shoulder muscles, lift your shoulders up toward your ears, hold, then release.

* Tense your arms, hold and release.

* Tighten your stomach and hips, hold and release.

* Clench your buttocks, hold and release.

* Tightly hold your thigh muscles, hold and release.

* Tighten your calf muscles, hold and release.

* Clench your feet, hold and release.

◊ Maintaining the focus on your body, are you still holding tension? Many people hold tension in their shoulders, which rise up toward the ears. Let your shoulder blades drop down to their natural place in your back, and feel the tension pouring away. Other people will grip with their toes, tense their stomach or wring their hands. Wherever you are hanging on to physical tension, breathe into it and let it go.

Dealing with your emotions

◊ Now turn your attention to your emotions. Identify them and examine them objectively. Acknowledge what they feel like, then cast them aside.

◊ Once you can look at each emotion dispassionately, without judgment, think about how it started and why you feel that way. What triggered it? What fueled it? What were the circumstances?

◊ Now that you understand the emotion, let go of the need to control it. Let it go and move on.

Conclusion

◊ Keep breathing deeply for a few minutes, then gradually bring your attention back into the room.

Developing your technique

If you find yourself thinking, "Well, that didn't seem to do much!", be patient.

For the lucky few, they may be in the right mindset to be successful the first time and feel an immediate benefit from meditation. You are very lucky. For most people, it takes a little time and perseverance before you begin to think it is having an effect. Be patient. Don't force it or try too hard. Just keep on going through the process and it will come.

You may find that simply focusing on the physical is the best way for you to start. That's fine. Try a few sessions just concentrating on relaxing your body until you really feel that you are in control of switching off all that tension. That alone will be doing you some good.

Always remember your breathing: keep it deep and slow. To help your timing, you might prefer not to count, but to say to yourself, "Breathe in for a count of five, breathe out for a count of five." That may be enough to get you started. Keep breathing and relaxing, and try to let yourself drift into a deeper contemplation. Trust that it will work, and be patient with yourself.

Try to maintain a regular routine, doing about 10 minutes of meditation every day. Don't extend the time until it feels natural to do so, and you start to feel that you're sinking into a deeper state of meditation. The regular commitment is the most important thing at this stage.

VISUALIZATION

Some people like to use visualization in their meditation. As the name suggests, this is acting out—in your mind—scenes and experiences. You can use it to work through things that have happened to you. It is also often helpful in confidence-building. One trick is to imagine someone you really admire and visualize how they might deal with a situation. Dramatizing the scene can give you insights into how it could be dealt with, and confirm that the way you handled it might have been better than you thought. Do not get attached to these visualizations; they are only a tool, and should not lead you away from the present moment.

"To be happy in the moment, that's enough. Each moment is all we need, not more."

MOTHER TERESA

7

EXPANDING INTO MINDFULNESS

When feelings of calm and positivity begin to seep out of your meditation routine and into your life, you're on your way to experiencing mindfulness. There is no hard-and-fast way to become mindful. Some people may instantly start to apply the principles to their lives at home, at work and in their social sphere. Others may find they have to keep it small to begin with. Whatever works for you and your circumstances is what is right.

Putting it into practice

"Drink your tea slowly and reverently,
as if it is the axis on which the
world earth revolves."
Thich Nhat Hanh

Sometimes it's easier to introduce mindfulness when you don't have to concentrate. What about when you're having a cup of tea? Really appreciate the flavors, the color, the warmth of the steam from the cup. When you're reading a book, totally immerse yourself in the story. If you're cooking a meal, appreciate the flavors and textures, the colors, and how everything blends together into the finished dish. Even walking down the street can be imbued with mindfulness as you feel the sidewalk beneath your feet and the wind on your face.

There are many ways to bring that level of awareness into your daily life. The next time you feel yourself slipping into feelings of being overwhelmed by thoughts, or constantly distracted by technological gadgets, take the time to stop and focus on just one thing, whatever that may be. It should be what you're doing right there and then or what you're feeling at that exact moment or even how your physical body feels.

Stop right now.

Contemplate your right hand. How does it feel? Is it itchy or swollen or tingly? Really look at the lines and small bumps and imperfections on it. What do your nails look like? What was the last thing you held in that hand?

If you don't remember, pick something up and really think about what it feels like. Where is the pressure? Does it feel smooth or rough? Try to use the technique to be mindful of your surroundings.

A-Z of mindful thinking

"The only thing that is ultimately real about your journey is the step that you are taking at this moment. That's all there ever is."
Eckhart Tolle

Here is an A to Z of things that are mindfulness-related. It includes techniques, ideas, and areas of your life that you might consider as a focus. There are some helpful tips to get you on your way, benefits, solutions to problems, and ideas to help you with all aspects of filling your life with mindfulness.

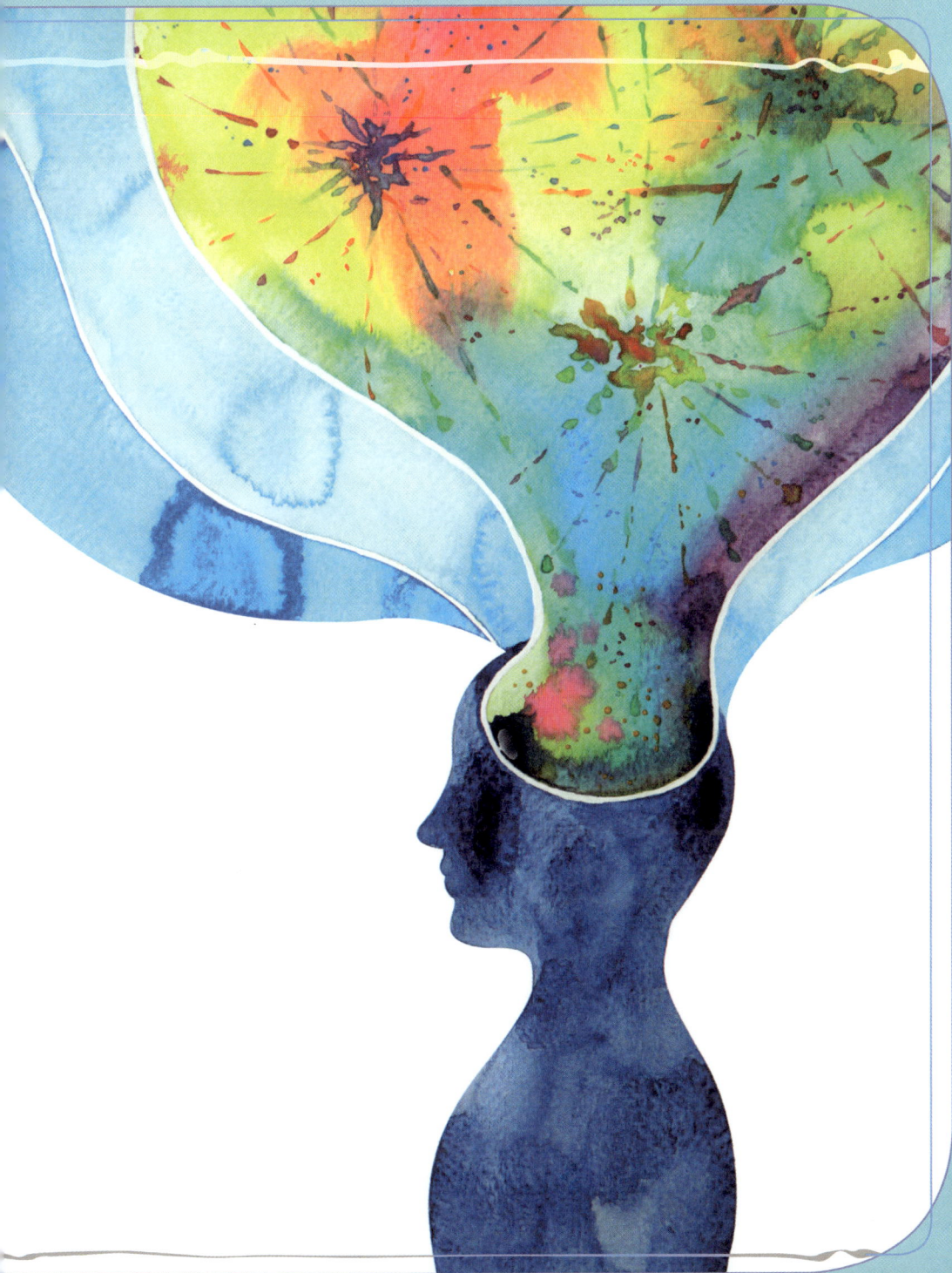

A is for...

Air

Some people find it beneficial to meditate in the open air; feeling the movement of the wind on their skin helps with focusing on the body in the present moment. It also makes deep breathing very effective.

Acknowledgment

There should be no judgment in feeling an emotion. If you feel angry, that is a fact, not an accusation; guilt or blame have no place there. If you can recognize what it feels like to be angry, acknowledge that you feel the emotion, then dismiss it. It does not control you, nor you it. Experience this with a range of emotions and you will find them easier to handle.

B is for...

Breathing

Slow, deep breathing is one of the most relaxing things you can do, and is an essential part of meditation. Breathe in slowly and deeply for a count of five, then breathe out fully for a count of five. If you find it hard to take such deep breaths to start with, then go as slowly as you reasonably can, and practice. You will find it easier with time. This is something you can do at any time of the day, when you need a break, when you feel anxious or tense, before you go to an important meeting, or if the kids ask for ice cream just one more time!

C is for...

Caring

Caring for others is important, and it is often the smallest of gestures that can give so much pleasure. So try not to miss the opportunity to pick up someone's glove, help them with their groceries or ask if they're okay if they trip. For every person who walks through the door you hold open for them without saying "thank you" (and, very unmindfully, I always say "thank you" to them, slightly louder than is necessary!), there are ten who will show that they are grateful.

Don't forget, though, that it is equally important to care for yourself. Look after your health—physical and mental—and make sure you have time to relax. Treat yourself now and then to a massage or an outing you will particularly enjoy.

D is for...

Decision-making

B ecause mindfulness helps you detach yourself from the raw emotions of any situation, it can help you make clearer decisions.

If something has happened that demands a decision—whether it is a disagreement with a partner, an offer of a job in a different city, or simply a choice of sofa—examining it during meditation can help you to balance what actually happened with how you felt about it. To take the simplest example, you want a red sofa but your partner favors blue. Perhaps you couldn't agree because each of you felt that they were being steamrolled into agreeing with the other person, and therefore both decided that they should stand their ground.

Looking at it dispassionately, it could be that one of you actually agrees with the other but was feeling it was their turn to make the choice. Acknowledge that and give in gracefully. Maybe neither color is right—consider another shade from the multicolored curtains that you both thought were great.

Whatever decision needs to be made, being able to look at it objectively will help you see both sides of the argument.

E is for...

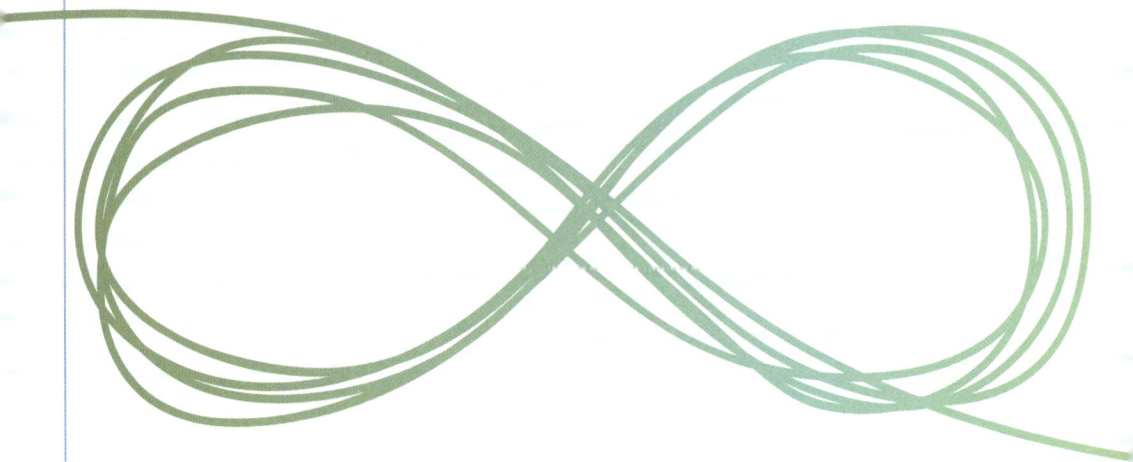

Ephemeral

E specially if you're experiencing a difficult stage of your life, there is a tendency to think it will go on forever, making the importance of the smallest detail grow out of all proportion in your mind. But change is one of the few reliable factors in life. Everything changes. Once you acknowledge this, you realize that whatever problems you are experiencing will change.

This can come as a great relief. If you can see that a solution will be found—that something will change—it can help soften the anxiety. This, in turn, could encourage you or give you the strength to move forward. Fear that you will be coping with the same problem endlessly can take over your thoughts to the exclusion of all else, freezing you into inaction because you keep circling the same ground. This is the opposite of what mindfulness is about. It can help you understand that each moment is precious, one leading to another in a constantly changing pattern.

F is for...

Fish

The myth that goldfish have a two-second memory would make them a mindfulness role model, if only it were true. Such a creature could only live in the moment, but there are other ways you can make them mindfulness allies. Watching their sinuous movements through the water is a good way to relax, while the detail of their scales and fins, and their fluid swimming motion, is great practice for being observant of the detail of things around you.

Fragrance

Some people like to use incense, flowers or a scented candle when they're meditating, because it can help them relax. Try different scents, but go for those that tend to be calming—such as lavender, ylang ylang, lemon, jasmine, rosemary or cinnamon.

G is for...

Gardening

Total absorption in the task at hand—whether that's digging, weeding, mowing or whatever—is perfect mindfulness territory. It's physical exercise that is healthy for you, working your muscles and allowing you the time to be completely aware of what you are doing. Add to that the beauty of the final results and you have a great combination.

If you follow your gardening with meditation, it can be a useful way to get into the right mindset and be one step ahead in your relaxation routine.

Guilt

Guilt is a highly corrosive emotion that often binds itself to other emotions like a parasitic plant, so it becomes difficult to separate the two. If you have been brought up to think that certain emotions are "bad," you're likely to feel guilt every time you feel those emotions. Try to separate the two when you are investigating your emotions during your meditation.

In a similar way, guilt can inveigle its way into your brain if you compare yourself too much to other people. If a friend has taken her parents on a vacation, you might feel guilty that you haven't done the same thing. But that is not a helpful place to be. Admit to yourself that you feel a little guilty, remember what it feels like, then discard it. What you do now in response to that knowledge is what matters.

H is for...

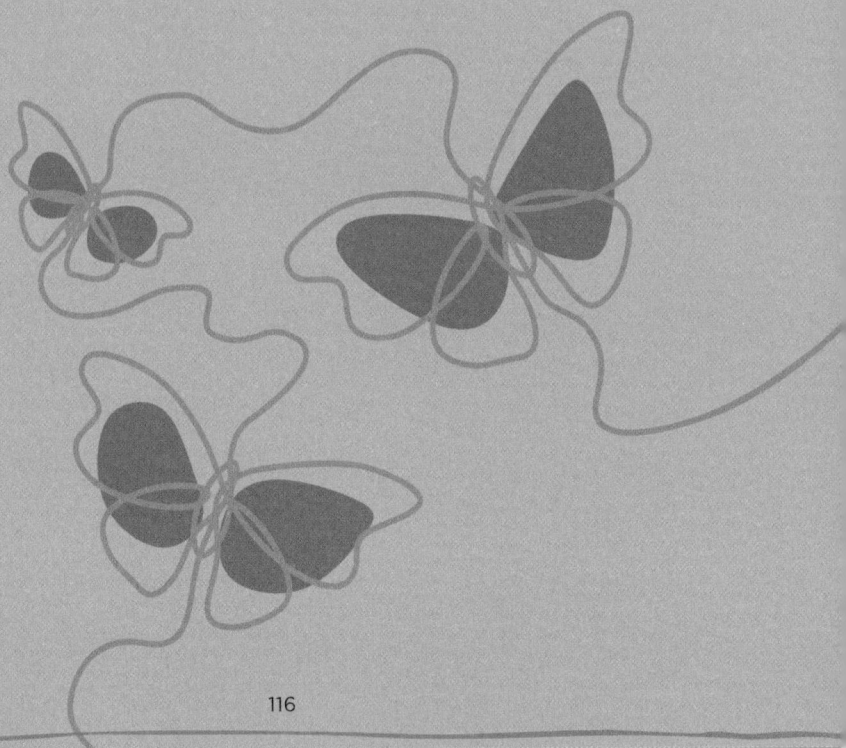

Holding on

Holding on to negative emotions leads only to churning over the same scenarios in your mind and not being able to free yourself from the ties of negativity.

Try choosing one emotion that you are hanging on to but no longer need—perhaps you have recently broken up with someone and are still wondering if it was the right thing to do. Go into your meditation and think about the emotions you feel. Identify what it is: sadness at the end of the relationship or for hopes dashed; anger after an argument; regret that you have made the wrong decision? Once you have identified the feeling, you may better understand how the situation worked out. You could also try thinking yourself into your partner's shoes; it might give you an insight on how your behavior affected them, and the reasons why you broke it off. Separate yourself from those emotions and look at the logic of your decision. You will probably find that you can see the decision more clearly and objectively.

I is for...

Imagination

Observation and visualization can both stimulate the imagination, a benefit that can be applied throughout life. Try visualizing a beautiful garden. Plot the layout, plant the trees, smell the flowers. Make it as extravagant as you wish, formal or informal, exotic or humble. Just give your imagination free rein. Take your time to enjoy the detail and, after all that work, revisit it as often as you like.

I am ...

You do not have to judge yourself—or be judged—by what you do. You are who you are—that's all. The more relaxed you are about being yourself, the more open you will be to other people. Dealing with negative emotions during meditation is a great way to achieve this level of understanding and self-confidence.

J is for...

Judgment

Whatever issue you are considering, if you are trying to judge yourself or someone else, you will be unlikely to find an equitable solution. Mindfulness refrains from judgment or blame. The incident has happened—it is what it is. Meditate. Step back. Look objectively at what happened, identify the emotion and how it made you feel, then put it behind you.

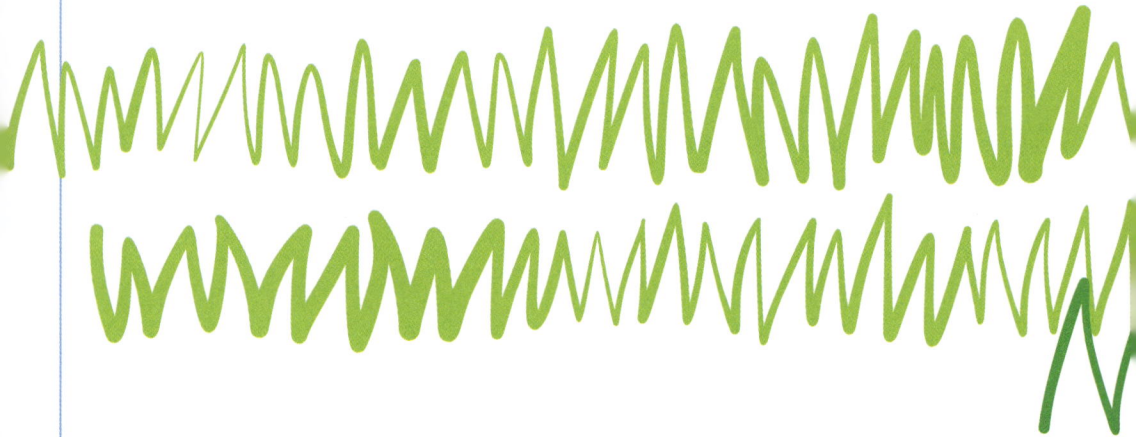

Jealousy

A common and corrosive emotion, the "green-eyed monster" can rear its head when you feel suspicious that you're being displaced by a rival. It can adversely color even the most innocent of circumstances or actions if you allow it to take hold. The first step is admitting that you are feeling jealousy; look at the circumstances that have triggered it and figure out why you're feeling jealous. If you have a good reason, perhaps an honest conversation with your partner is in order.

Jealousy is often confused with envy, but they are not the same. Envy is when you begrudge or desire something that someone else possesses. It is no less destructive, and can be treated in the same way.

K is for...

Kaleidoscope

A kaleidoscope can be a metaphor for the myriad thoughts that are moving around your brain at any one time, from mundane daytime activities to work projects or looking forward to a vacation or thinking about an outing.

But remember that you are in control of how the patterns change. If you keep turning the dial, the pieces will keep shifting and the patterns will keep changing until you can no longer think straight. If you keep still and observe, you can really appreciate the beauty of that instant, then move on in your own time.

L is for...

Lighting

Some seasoned meditators will be able to meditate in any circumstances. Others find atmosphere important, and a priority there can be lighting. Bright sunlight, dappled shade, dim indoor lighting or darkness—all of these can make a difference to your ability to find a meditative state. Try different things until you find what works best for you.

M is for...

Music

Noise—or the absence of it—is important to many people when they are meditating.

Absolute silence is many people's first choice, but others prefer subtle, natural sounds—like birdsong—or soft, rhythmic music. A rhythmic beat is conducive to helping you relax, although avoiding anything too heavy or strident makes sense. Lose yourself in the music and use it to help you meditate.

N is for...

Nature observation

We are all part of the natural world, and learning more about it and how we interact with it is something many people find both calming and sustaining. Even if you're a city-dweller, there must be somewhere you can go where there is a little green. Go for a walk in the park, by the river or in the countryside. There will be so much to see that if you are learning to be more observant, you may not know where to start—there is nowhere you need to stop!

So start with a leaf—or any other small item you might pick up. Give it all your attention. Look at the color, the patterns; feel the texture, the lightness; how does it bend; how does it fall through the air? Absorb your concentration in it completely.

This is a great practice for improving your observation skills in everyday life, so you really begin to notice things and can use it to enhance your life and improve your relationship with others. Comment on the new shirt your partner is wearing—they'll be pleased you noticed. Enjoy the rose bush you pass every day on your way to work and see it budding, blooming, then fading. Notice when a friend is unhappy and invite them over for coffee. Observe when they are looking particularly buoyant— did they get that new job? Watch and learn.

O is for...

Overthinking

This is the root cause of the vicious cycle that we can so easily become embroiled in. If something has made you angry or upset, and you feel you could have acted in a different way, do you keep going over it in your head, replaying what you should have said (or not said), blaming yourself for not showing your true feelings, blaming the other person for how they spoke or acted?

What good does it do? You can feel yourself in that circular motion, hanging on to the negative energy and letting the conflict take control.

Meditate. Take yourself to the edge of the conflict and look at it as though you were looking at someone else. Acknowledge that this is what has happened and you cannot change it. Forgive yourself and the other person involved so you can move on. Calmly decide whether you need to take action, and what to do but, because you have defused the situation, it no longer has control over you.

"Take away the complaint, 'I have been harmed,' and the harm is taken away," is one of the most quoted statements of Roman Emperor Marcus Aurelius.

P is for...

Peer pressure

Are you a label junkie? Are your children under pressure to have the latest gadgets or branded goods? This is a complex and difficult modern phenomenon, especially in design and technology. There are no simple solutions, but you may be able to start—perhaps saving some money could be an incentive—by trying to take a mindful approach. Try to mindfully consider the things you need and those you would like. Get pleasure from them when you wear them, carry them, use them or look at them. If a designer outfit is uncomfortable and doesn't make you feel good, ask whether it is worth the cost. Do you really want it? Does it make you feel good about who you are or who you think you should be?

If you are not true to yourself, you may not find the contentment you are looking for, because it could be the "things" and what they represent that you are seeking, rather than the personal pleasure they bring you. Treat yourself when you can; having beautiful things that give you pleasure, and giving gifts of great or small value but of emotional importance, all contribute to our happiness.

When you are choosing to buy anything for yourself or your home, think about its value to you and how it represents your personality, not about what others will think of it.

Q is for...

Quiet

Valuing and appreciating silence is a subtle art, because nothing is truly silent. You might hear the wind in the trees, the ripple of water, the cry of a bird or the clatter of stones on a beach. It might be the sound of a car, a closing door or a smartphone. Appreciate the variations and how from each one you can learn a little more about focusing and meditating.

Quality time

The time you spend with those closest to you is quality time—treat it as such. Forget distractions and anything else on your to-do list and focus on enjoying the time you have with them. This is particularly true of older relatives. Spend quality time with them, let them talk about their past and their experiences—it is probably their No. 1 interest—so you can learn about the history of your family. The more you learn, the more fascinated you are likely to be with the personal and social changes they have witnessed during their lifetime.

R is for...

Rest

While it is true that the brain behaves differently when sleeping than when awake or meditating, you can still use mindfulness to obtain a restful state. Sleep is important to maintain our health and well-being. If you find it difficult to sleep, it may be worth having your meditation session just before you go to bed so you're in a relaxed and calm frame of mind, ready to fall into a deep and nourishing sleep.

S is for...

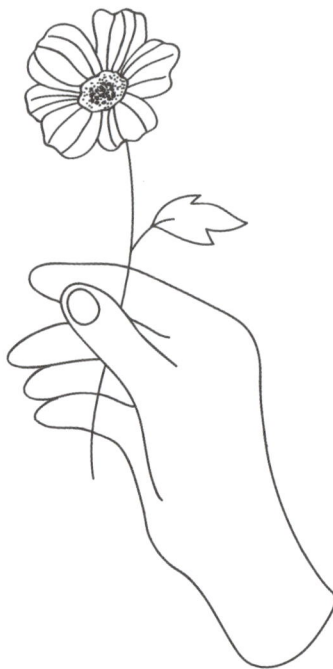

Sensory awareness

Undertake an exercise in concentration by choosing an object that you find interesting: perhaps a stone, a flower, or a cobweb. Concentrate on the object; observe it in all its detail. Try to block everything else out of your mind and become completely absorbed in that thing in that moment. This is a great way of getting into the feeling of meditation.

T is for...

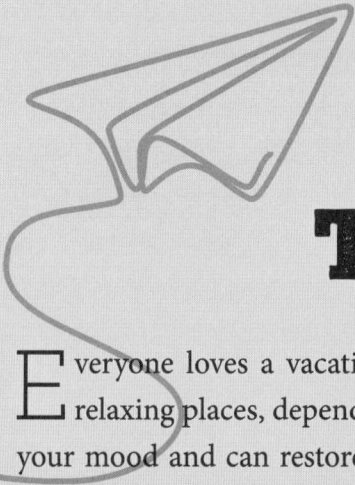

Travel

Everyone loves a vacation, and to get away to exotic, inspiring or relaxing places, depending on the type of break you prefer. They lift your mood and can restore your positive energies. So it's possible that when you return to your normal routine, it seems dull and gradually becomes more oppressive. You could exist from one vacation to the next and come alive only for a few weeks each year.

But if you practice mindfulness, you will be able to recall experiences in detail and relive them in your imagination when you return home, making a vacation a treasured memory that will last forever. You can also use your meditation to travel in your mind, not just visualizing and reliving the beauty you have already seen, but creating imaginative scenarios that will energize and sustain you.

Because mindfulness helps you feel at one with the universe, the relaxation and contentment it brings gives you a more realistic focus on the wonders of the life you have, because your eyes are on the moment and your oneness with everything around you in that moment, rather than the recurring thought that the grass is always greener on the other side.

U is for...

Unbalanced

When you're thinking about ways to improve your life, you are always looking for balance. If you are working long hours and always seem to be obsessed with work, allowing no time for friends or just chilling out, it is clearly an unbalanced lifestyle. The solution is often obvious, but rarely easy to implement. Think about your options, trying to view the situation dispassionately, and gradually work toward what is the right balance for you at the time.

V is for...

Vicious circle

By definition, circular thinking will get you nowhere. If you are fixated on things that have happened in the past and reliving them over and over, the result will almost certainly be that you will start to expect every situation to turn out in the same way. Obviously, the more negative the outcome in the past, the bigger a negative impact it is going to have on the present.

Similarly, those who project into a future which, by definition, is unknown, cannot resolve a problem because the future, by definition, is uncertain.

By dwelling only in the present, you can address an issue dispassionately, giving you the best chance of making an informed but balanced decision. And you will replace the vicious with the virtuous circle: satisfaction > appreciation > contentment > gratitude > satisfaction.

Visualization

V isualization is a great tool to boost your self-confidence. Start with your usual route into meditation, then focus on a scenario that has played out in your life but that did not end as successfully as you hoped. Now imagine someone you admire—it can be someone you know or someone famous—going through the same situation and imagine how they would have acted.

Keep replaying the scene, but take back your own role so you see yourself coping with the situation with calm confidence. Next time you encounter a similar situation, you will be better prepared to deal with it.

W is for...

Walking

For general health and exercise, walking is a good way to get out and do some gentle exercise. If you can combine it with interesting surroundings, it gives you an opportunity to practice your new skill of observation, too. Whatever your environment—rural or urban—there will be things to keep your mind occupied. At some point on your walk, stop and reflect for a few moments. Focus on one thing you have found of interest, or focus on nothing and just relax. Look for beauty in all things.

X is for...

Xenophile

A xenophile is someone who loves foreign things and people, so introduce the world to your inner xenophile and get curious about the people and objects that are foreign to your experience. When you practice meditation, you need to open your mind to new experiences, to change, and to a broadening of your life. This open-mindedness then extends to every aspect of your life and allows you to simply be curious about uncomfortable things that happen, rather than reacting to them immediately with anger or fear.

This might be a call to try something new, to look for a new understanding of yourself and what you need in life to make you feel contented.

Y is for...

Yoga

Part of the practice of yoga is that it encompasses body, mind and spirit and unites them in meditation and physical practice. It is similar to meditation, but the focus is maintained through the control of the body in the sequence of movements and holds.

There are many different types of yoga, each with its own style. If you have seen yoga practitioners holding bizarre positions for a considerable length of time and been put off, investigate other yoga styles. There's likely to be one that works for you.

Z is for...

Zen

Zen is a school of Buddhism that developed in China in the 6th century, having been introduced by the Indian monk Bodhidharma. It has since split into several subdivisions under Mahayana Buddhism. While meditation is important in all forms of Buddhism, it is especially crucial in Zen Buddhism; one of the main tenets of the discipline is that you should not worry about anything over which you have no influence. The word itself has therefore come to mean calm and relaxed, a person who is able to rise above conflict, never lose their temper and always be contented.

"The little things?
The little moments?
They aren't little."

JON KABAT-ZINN

8
YOUR NEW MINDFUL LIFE

*How far have you come? You can always continue to improve,
but if you are successfully beginning to discover mindfulness for yourself,
then you will understand the quotations and begin to find that
you can absorb the energy of the moment, and that will energize
you and help you grow in contentment.*

Review your progress

After you have been meditating regularly for a little while, reassess the things you thought about when you started out. Think about the assessment of your own character, about what you felt you could improve, and where you thought changes would be most obviously felt.

Were you correct? How much have you achieved? Do you feel the outcomes that were predicted, or are they more or less different from what you anticipated?

Try to retain your state of mindfulness with regular meditation. Feel the immediate benefits and develop your skills at applying the principles in life situations. Above all, feel the contentment of knowing yourself better and knowing that you are making the best of yourself. Live each day— don't just exist as it passes by—and you will wring from it every iota of joy.

The ultimate aim is to be happy with yourself and make the most of your life. If your approach is secular, you'll want to make this one and only life as good as it can be. If you are a person of faith—any faith—then making this life a good one will lead you on to a better spiritual experience.

Further reading

BOOKS

Assessing Mindfulness, Michael Treadway and Sara Lazar

Blue Sky Mind, Ian Gawler

Brain and Cognition, Jessica Stillman

Buddha''s Brain: The Practical Neuroscience of Happiness, Love and Wisdom, Rick Hanson

Conscious Creativity, Philippa Stanton

Headspace, Andy Puddicombe

How to Find Peacefulness, Tina Jefferies

Idiot's Guide to Mindfulness, Donya Sater Burk

Psychology Today, 'Use your mind to change your brain', 'You are not your brain', Rebecca Gladding MD

The Mind Illuminated, Dr John Yate

The Yoga Handbook, Noa Belling

Unstuck, Tim Lane

ONLINE RESOURCES

bemindful.co.uk

iangawler.com

mindful.org

mindfulspot.com

pursuit-of-happiness.org

zenhabits.net

Chakras

Chakras

How to focus the energy points of the body

Julian Flanders

ARCTURUS

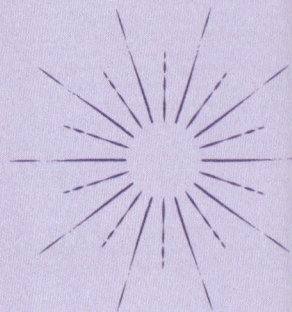

ARCTURUS

This edition published in 2021 by Arcturus Publishing Limited
26/27 Bickels Yard, 151–153 Bermondsey Street,
London SE1 3HA

ISBN: 978-1-3988-1319-9
AD007322US

Printed in China

Contents

Introduction
What are chakras?

The word chakra is derived from the Sanskrit word *cakra*, meaning "wheel" or "circle." Inside our bodies, we have a number of whirling, vortex-like centers of natural energy that, taken together, form a channel for the integration of mind, body and spirit. This invisible energy, often called *prana*, is our life force and, when in balance, keeps us vibrant, healthy and alive.

It is important to understand that chakras have no physicality, but, corresponding to nerve centers in the body, they act like water currents directing energy up and down the body and around the major organs. There are seven main chakras, which start at the base of the spine and go up to the crown of the head. They sit in the subtle body (see pages 19-21) at points where matter and consciousness meet, providing us with a connecting channel between our minds and our bodies, our physical being and our spiritual selves, the past, the present and the future. In this way, the chakras can have an influence on both our physical and our emotional lives.

In her book *Wheels of Life*, Anodea Judith suggests that "chakras are organizing centers for the reception, assimilation and transmission of life energies." Although the human body is an amazing machine, performing incredible feats every day, from sending signals rocketing through the brain at high speed to distributing oxygen over 1,000 miles (1,600 kilometers) of airways, it can do nothing without energy. Judith sees the chakras as "the wheels of life that carry [us] through trials, tribulations and transformations."

Given the way chakras can be said to govern our lives, it is essential that they remain open, aligned and fluid. Because mind and body are completely interrelated, one blocked chakra is likely to affect another. These blockages can be: physical, such as a tumor, a cyst, a stomach ache or a sore throat; emotional, perhaps in the form of anxiety or depression; psychological, spiritual, karmic or energetic. It will also depend on which chakra is blocked. For example, if your third chakra is affected, then you might experience a lack of confidence or self-esteem, indigestion, shame or an allergic reaction. If your fifth chakra is blocked, then you might find it difficult to communicate ideas, or you may suffer from a lack of creativity, or from problems with your neck or shoulders.

In any spiritual practice, awareness is the first step toward healing. For some, this means stepping out of the dark into the light; for others, it means realizing that you have gained weight and that you must do something about it. The aim of this book is to make you aware of your chakras and how they can have a positive effect on your life. There are chapters on each of the chakras, how to open and balance them through meditation and yoga, how to feed them, and how to heal them if they become blocked.

Part One

THE CHAKRAS

The history of chakras

The concept of chakras originally came from ancient India. The first references are found in the *Vedas* (which literally means "knowledge") and the *Upanishads* (see page 12). Now regarded as some of the most sacred scripts of Hinduism, these are collections of religious texts, poems, prayers, songs and stories. They include material that had been transmitted orally over many generations among the local population of north-western India, including the Sanskrit-speaking Aryans from the Indus valley. As the dominant language of the region, these texts were written in the Aryan language.

Although the authorship of the texts is unclear, the worldview, social attitudes and spiritual preoccupations recorded tend to reflect those of the Brahmans, the priestly class, of ancient India. They also hint at the beginnings of the caste system in the region, at the top of which sat the Brahmans, above the Kshatriyas (warriors), the Vaishyas (landowners and merchants) and the Shudras (laborers). It seems logical, even from this distance, that those who controlled the writing and distribution of texts such as these would be the dominant caste in such a primitive society.

However, the word *cakra* used in these ancient texts did not refer to psychic energy centers, but rather to a circle, as in a seasonal cycle or the wheel of time. It was also used in a political sense, referring to the wheel of a chariot, symbolic of political power and influence. The use of the term to indicate energy vortices first appeared much later, in medieval Hindu and Buddhist texts.

COMMUNICATING WITH THE GODS

At that time (the *Vedas* were written between 1500 and 1200 BCE), India was an agricultural society, dependent on water and the natural cycle of the seasons. The people believed in many gods and spirits, often relating to natural forces, such as storms, wind and fire, and included those living in animals, trees, rivers and mountains. Some of the gods were good and others bad, but the most revered were those chosen by the Vedic priests. The myths surrounding the gods, such as Indra, the god of storms and of war, and Agni, the god of fire and soma, who was the personification of the soma plant—whose holy

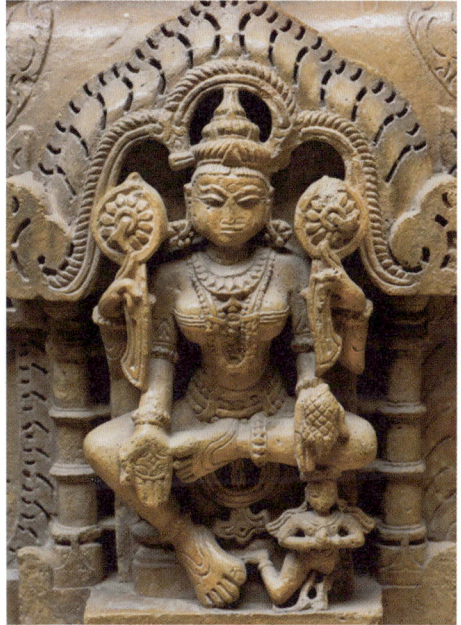

Sandstone relief of the tantric meditation deity, the goddess Tara, at a 12th-century Jain temple in Rajasthan, India.

juice was intoxicating to both gods and men—provided the link between humans and the gods.

In order to communicate with the gods to maintain the balance of the cosmos, the priests would conduct rituals and sacrifices. To perform these sacred ceremonies, the priests had to reach a state of bliss. They did this through meditation in which they held poses that would open their bodies and minds to the deities; it is claimed that these poses are the earliest examples of yoga. The priests hoped that in return for these rituals and sacrifices, the gods would offer protection from the bad spirits.

REJECTION OF THE VEDIC TRADITION

However, as nature is not dependent on rituals, when things went wrong and rain washed out the crops, or drought occurred, people would question the priests' intentions. Some sense of the rejection of priestly ideas and religious practices appeared in new texts published as the *Upanishads* (*c.* 900 BCE). Somewhere around the beginning of the 7th century BCE, a new culture of world-renunciation began, shifting the focus of religious life away from rights and sacrifices that were rejected as they did not work. Although adherents to this new system retained certain elements of previous practice, notably meditation and yoga, their spiritual quests for truth became internal rather than external. The priests condemned these new ideas as "heretical," but over time religion in the Vedic tradition was rejected and replaced by new movements, such as Charvaka, Jainism and Buddhism, that originated around this time.

THE CLASSIC CHAKRA SYSTEMS

Most historians agree that Hinduism, which developed between 500 BCE and 300 CE, is where the concepts of chakras as part of ancient meditation practices, known as *Tantra* (see pages 15-18), originated. A theory developed suggesting that human life had two parallel dimensions, one physical (the mass of the human body) and the other non-physical (energy or the subtle body), which interacted with each other. The subtle body (see pages 19-21) consisted of *nadi* (energy channels), which circulated around the body. The focal points at which this interaction took place were known as *chakras*. The number of chakras believed to be present in a human body varied widely, but the main ones, normally believed to be between four and seven, were arranged along the spinal cord. Tantric traditions developed, seeking to awaken the chakras and energize them through meditation and breathing techniques. The chakras, though not

A young priest sits in meditation under a banyan tree—such practices are used to achieve a state of bliss and communion with the gods.

physical in form, were mapped and matched to a person's psychological state, sounds, deities, colors and other motifs.

These traditions varied widely within Hinduism and there were similar ideas in other cultures too, notably Chinese medicine, Tibetan Buddhism, Jewish Kabbalah, Malayan and Indonesian metaphysical theory, among others. They all shared the concept of a "life energy" and the existence of psycho-spiritual "organs" or faculties, the activation of which make a person complete. Traditional Chinese Medicine relied on a similar model of the human body as an energy system; Tantric Buddhism emphasized "organic harmony," often achieved through yoga; the Kabbalah believed the key to spirituality was self-awareness, achieved by connecting the physical body and its etheric counterpart; while the Silat tradition of the Malay Archipelago believed that defensive and offensive energy rotates through the body along diagonal lines.

Tantra

Tantra is a word originally used to denote early esoteric traditions of Hindu and Buddhist adherents, and it is the source of the concept of chakras. Many of these traditions centered around deities such as Vishnu, the "Supreme Being," Shiva and Shakti. Believers held that all realities were the product of the relationship between Shakti, the mother of the universe, and Shiva, the energy of all existence. She the life-giver; he formless until given life. Early tantric texts often took the form of conversations between the two deities, which revealed how much they depended on one another. Arthur Avalon explains the relationship in his book *The Serpent Power* (see page 28): "There is no power-holder without power. No power without power-holder. Power is Shakti, the Great Mother of the

An illustration depicting the union of Shiva and Shakti energy through the chakras.

universe. There is no Shiva without Shakti, or Shakti without Shiva."

Shiva and Shakti are often depicted in statues and images in a constant embrace, creating the universe through their love, much as life is created by a woman using the man's seed. The intention of their union was also to achieve a state of bliss. But as well as creating life, the two are seen as forming a bridge between the earthly (Shakti) and the divine (Shiva), between the body and the spirit, between the Earth and heaven. This concept of balance is further reflected in the idea that the energy passing through the chakras in our bodies flows both upward and downward; it moves down to feed the body and soul, and up toward creativity and freedom. Tantric traditions also embraced the elements: earth, fire, air, water and space (ether), which are regarded as the raw materials of existence. It is because of this that each chakra is associated with one of the elements.

One of the earliest tantric belief systems was Shaivism. First recorded in the Kashmir Valley from about 600 BCE, it is one of the earliest sources of postural asana yoga practices. This was followed by hatha yoga, which can be traced back to around 1100 BCE. Since then, tantric traditions have developed in many Eastern religions, from Jainism and Shinto to Daoism and Tibetan Bön, examples of which are often seen in temple building, artworks and other imagery throughout Southeast Asia.

The use of the word tantra to refer to all esoteric practice and ritual is an invention from colonial-era Europe. The term, which means "loom," was used as a metaphor for weaving separate threads into one whole entity, creating the fabric of existence, linking mind and body, man and woman, the physical and the spiritual.

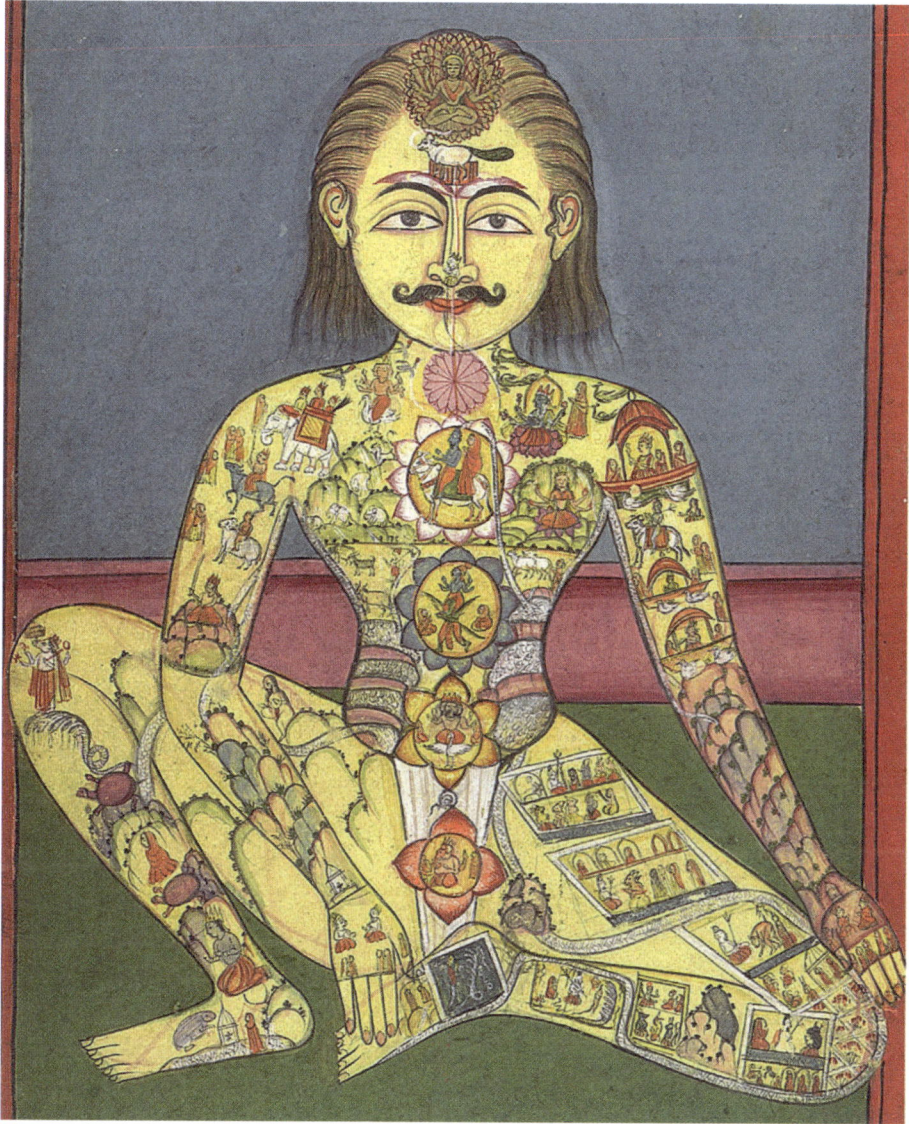

Illustration from a 19th-century yoga manuscript in the Braja-bhasa language depicting the chakras and energetic correspondences of the body.

In the early years of the 20th century, a yogi and occultist called Pierre Bernard began introducing and monetizing the philosophy and practices of tantra to his native America. He did raise its profile, but a series of scandals centering around his schools for teaching what he called "mystical sex techniques" saw him discredited, and created a misleading impression of its connection to sex, an impression that still survives today. Modern tantric practices do contain a sexual element, normally associated with the goddess Kundalini, as one way of achieving bliss, though this can equally be obtained through celibacy. Tantric practices, including yoga, meditation and caring for your chakras, are other ways to achieve liberation. In tantra, the body is a temple and should be kept purified and healthy through yoga, breathing techniques and a healthy diet—things that will help ensure sexual pleasure.

Of course, tantra is more than that. According to Sanskrit scholar and tantric teacher Christopher Wallis, "Tantra is fundamentally a world-embracing rather than world-denying [philosophy]. It focuses on the imminent rather than the transcendent, integrating with everyday life rather than renouncing it." For him, the tantric view is that the world and everything in it is an expression of the divine, and that seeking a deeper awareness of it all, through tantra, leads to realization.

The subtle body

Chakras do not exist physically in the body; they exist in something called the subtle body, which comprises a number of vibrating energy fields that surround every living thing, from a cell to a plant to a human being. Together these bands of energy make up the auric field. Experts argue about the number of fields present around a human body (some say six, some seven and others twelve), but they do agree that these fields overlay our physical selves and provide a space for interaction between mind and body. They regulate all our physical and spiritual functions in correspondence with various parts of the subtle body.

A corona of light, or halo, around Jesus Christ and his disciples is believed by some to depict the subtle body and its external manifestation in the aura.

The physical body generates energy that vibrates slowly; in this way it appears to our physical eyes to be solid. As you move out from the physical body to the invisible layers of the auric field, which includes the etheric body, the emotional body, the mental body, the astral body, the etheric template body, the celestial body and the causal body (sometimes referred to as the ketheric template), each field vibrates slightly faster than the previous one. Each of these layers connect to the physical body via energy points—the chakras—which direct energy into the physical body via the *nadis* and the meridian system.

The term "subtle body" is used in a number of esoteric teachings including Hinduism, Buddhism and Jainism, and there are a number of different theories about the importance of these auric layers. Some define the subtle body as that part of our being or consciousness that leaves our body at the time of physical death. Others describe it as the part of the body that perceives sensation—for example, where amputees feel "pain" or "itching" in their missing limbs. Another theory is that it includes the subtle sense organs (the aspect of our five sense organs with which we are able to perceive the subtle realm) and the subtle motor organs (all activity in our physical motor organs is first initiated in our subtle motor organs).

Perhaps the most outlandish theory came from the scientist Rupert Sheldrake in the early 1980s. He suggested that a "morphogenetic" layer was also present in the auric field. In biology, a morphogenic field is a group of cells that lead to specific tissues or organs, and that because only living organisms that belong to a certain group can tune in to a particular morphic resonance. In this way, a dog, for example, would not develop the characteristics of a plant, and so on.

Sheldrake took the idea further, suggesting that the morphogenic field might actually sit alongside DNA in explaining how certain behaviors, characteristics and emotions are carried down through a family, particularly when separated by time and space. His theory was that past-life memories could pass from lifetime to lifetime through a soul's morphic energy field. These memories would be non-local, and not anchored in the brain or in a particular life. This could explain, for example, how a granddad's talent as a fine artist was carried on to his grandson.

Taken together, the layers of the auric field make up what is more popularly known as the aura.

The aura

T he aura is the external manifestation of the subtle body, an "energy skin" that protects the energy of the human body much as physical skin protects the inner organs. It surrounds the body like an egg-shaped cocoon. This phenomenon has been recognized by many cultures and religions throughout history, including the coronas of light around Jesus and his disciples in Christian iconography, the Kabbalist tradition of astral light, and in the teachings of the Vedic scriptures.

A human's aura is created by the action of the life-force energy, *prana*, within the body. It resonates through the chakras and both the physical and subtle anatomy. The auric field is similar to an electromagnetic field emanating from an electrical device. It can be perceived as color, brightness, shape or density. Some can hear it as sound or vibration, and others can feel the aura's energy through heartbeat or body temperature.

Someone's auric color reflects their current energy status, often appearing in multiple layers of various rainbow colors. Many things can affect the shade of each layer of color, from simple things like mood to more major issues such as spiritual development. It can change from minute to minute or remain a steady shade and intensity for longer periods of time.

If you have ever met a professional athlete, you might have noticed the power and strength emanating from them, indicating an aura at its peak of health. If someone is healthy, self-confident, calm and grounded, their aura will be clean and brightly colored; they will emanate strong vibrations and strong tones, and will have a full, smoothly shaped boundary. In contrast, the aura of someone who is ill, depressed or unsure of him or herself would be thinner and dull-colored. Its vibrations would be slow and even erratic, and it might have a break or tear in the boundary.

Because the aura has been such a universally accepted phenomenon for so long, there has been a considerable amount of scientific investigation into its mysteries, particularly since the 1880s. An early theory, posited by Jan Baptist van Helmond, suggested that it acted like a fluid. This was further developed by Franz Mesmer, of "mesmerism" fame, who suggested that both animate and inanimate objects were

A colored etching depicting a scene in which a number of patients in Paris receive Mesmer's animal magnetism therapy.

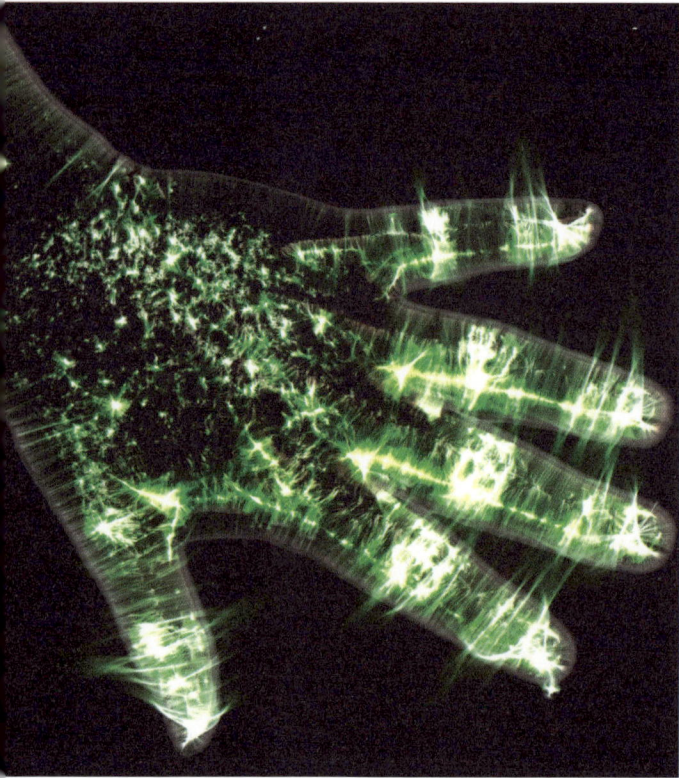

Baron Wilhelm von Reichenbach was the first to relate the human energy field to different colors, which Kirlian photography later made visible to the eye.

charged with a magnetic fluid by which material bodies could exert influence over each other. Baron Wilhelm von Reichenbach was the first to relate the human energy field to different colors. He agreed that the aura could carry a charge, and described the field on the left-hand side of the body as a negative pole and the right as positive. This idea is mirrored in Chinese medicine.

A particular area of interest has also been how to "see" auras, since clairvoyance, though effective and enormously popular in the Victorian era, was not evidence enough for many skeptics. In 1911, Dr Walter Kilner conducted an experiment that established the connection between the auric energy field and the human body. Using specially designed goggles, he was able to see a patient's aura and detect a shift in the condition of it in reaction to their state of mind and their health. He proposed its use in medical diagnosis and prognosis.

In the 1930s, research began to focus on what were then called "bio-currents" emanating from the human body. Russian scientists were able to measure energy fields, discovering that living organisms emanate vibrations at a frequency between 300 and 2,000 nanometers. Another development occurred in Russia when scientists Semyon and Valentina Kirlian developed a process that involved directing a high-frequency electrical field at someone and then taking photographs. The photos revealed the person's pattern of luminescence—their auric energy field. Practitioners today still use Kirlian photography to reveal patients' emotional and mental states, and even to diagnose illnesses and other problems.

In 1988, computer technology enabled Dr Valerie Hunt to record electrical signals emanating from the human body during Rolfing (a type of alternative healing bodywork) sessions with her patients. The wave patterns were then analyzed, and revealed that the energy fields did actually consist of different colored bands, which in all cases correlated with the colors associated with the chakras. The slowest, measured in hertz, was blue; it was followed by green, yellow, orange, red, violet and white. Dr Hunt took things a little further, inviting a psychic to use intuitive perception to figure out the aura of the same patients. In all cases, the renderings produced were the same as those demonstrated by the technology.

Part Two

THE SEVEN-CHAKRA SYSTEM

A brief guide

Although they are all originally from the same tantric tradition, there have been five-chakra, six-chakra, seven-, nine-, ten-, twelve-, twenty-one and more chakra systems taught throughout history. There are major chakras, usually corresponding to parts of the spine, and a multitude of lesser chakras—for example, in your hands, feet, joints and back. But it is the Shakta seven-chakra system that is now commonly accepted in the West. The history of this system goes back to a 10th-century text, the *Kubjika-mata-tantra*, which taught a system incorporating six major chakras arranged along the axial channel of the human body, with a seventh point at the top, not then regarded as a chakra.

The popularity of this system was boosted in the early years of the 20th century through the publication of a book called *The Serpent Power*, written by British orientalist Sir John Woodroffe (also known as Arthur Avalon) in 1918. This was a translation of the *Sat-cakra-nirupana*, a Sanskrit text written in 1577 by Purnananda Yati. This was followed in 1927 by an even more remarkable book, *The Chakras*, by Charles Webster Leadbeater, a prominent clairvoyant and theosophist, in which the author described each of the by-then seven chakras in exquisite detail, including its placement on the body, size, shape, colors and even vibratory pulsations. He also illustrated each "circle," painting them, as he claims, from detailed accounts of individuals who were able to see the chakras using clairvoyant powers.

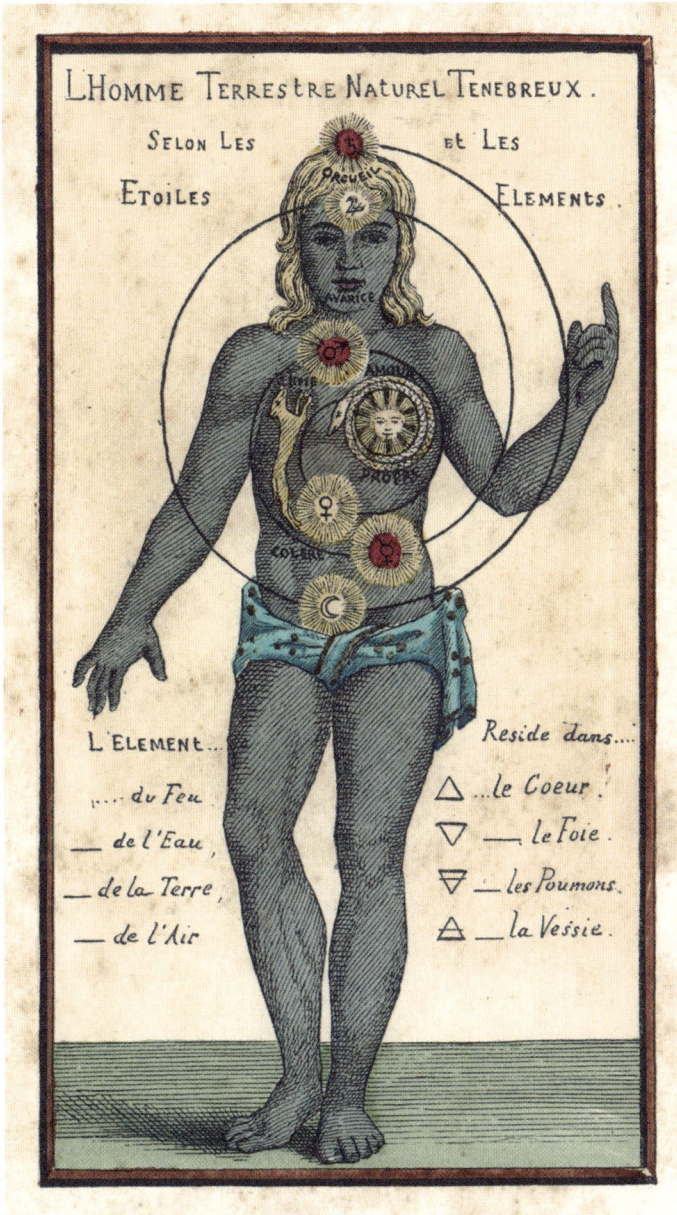

The chakras according to Johann Georg Gichtel, showing the four elements and where they reside in the body.

Purist critics are often dubious about the provenance of these works, claiming that the chakra concept today bears little resemblance to that originally envisaged in the *Vedas* and *Upanishads,* and pointing out that many of its elements are incorrect and some are even untrue. However, while the seven-chakra system is only one of many models, and has many elements that have been added in recent years, meaning that it bears little resemblance to the ancient practices on which it is based, this is the system that has been adopted in the West and throughout the world. Perhaps even more persuasive is the fact that present-day Indian gurus also use this theory in their system of philosophy and teachings.

According to

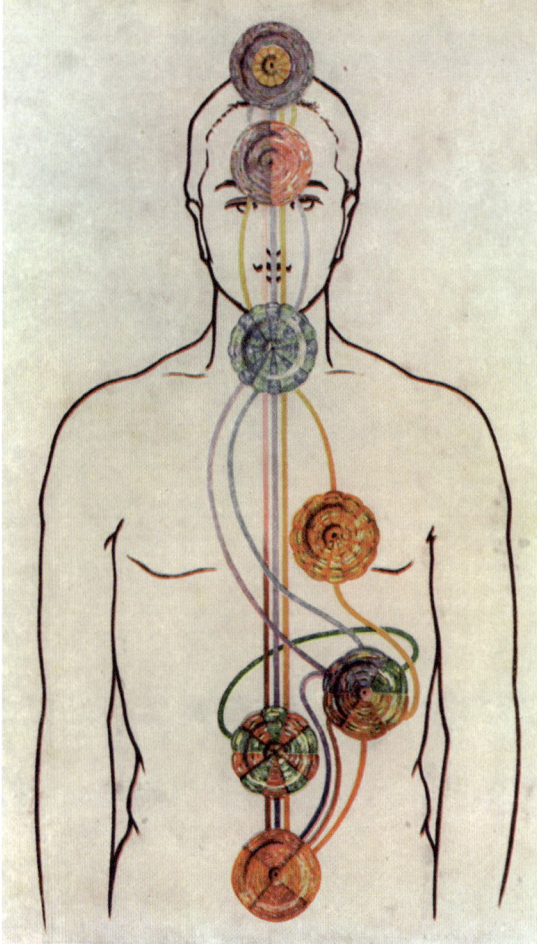

The positioning of the seven chakras according to Charles Webster Leadbeater.

Christopher Wallis, however, there are certain elements of current Western teaching about chakras that do come from original sources. Chakras are visualized as lotus flowers, with a different number of petals in each one. The mystical sounds of the Sanskrit alphabet are associated with the lotus petals of each of the chakras in the system. This is helpful in the meditation used to open each chakra, providing a template for *nyasa* ("placing") by giving you a specific mantric syllable to access a specific chakra by silently, or otherwise, intoning its sound.

Each chakra is also associated with a specific element (earth, water, fire, wind and space), its relevant color, and a specific Hindu deity or deities. The seven chakras are described as being aligned in an ascending column along the major nerve ganglia from the base of the spine to the top of the head. In modern practice, each chakra is associated with a certain color. Chakras are associated with multiple physiological functions, an aspect of consciousness, a classical element, and other distinguishing characteristics. These are all included in the chapters on each chakra that follow later on in the book in order to give you as complete a picture as possible of each chakra.

Below are brief descriptions of the seven chakras and their main characteristics. Before reading, it is important to remember that chakras are not "things." As Lar Short, co-author of *The Body of Light*, a seminal book on the inner workings of all spiritual traditions, says, "You cannot cut open a yogi and find chakras, any more than you can dissect an opera singer and find librettos and songs." But they do exist within the subtle body, exhibiting a strong influence on such things as body shape, health, well-being and wholeness.

Muladhara (see page 36)

The root chakra, also known as the base chakra, is located at the base of the spine. It helps keep the energy of the body grounded and connected with earthly energies. Helps movement, survival and self-esteem.

Svadhisthana (see page 48)

The sacral chakra is located in the lower abdomen, between the navel and the genitals; this chakra is associated with your kidneys, bladder, circulatory system, and reproductive organs and glands. It is concerned with emotion and represents desire, pleasure, sexuality, procreation and creativity.

Manipura (see page 60)

The solar plexus chakra seeks to achieve balance in self-esteem issues and intuitive skills. This chakra is associated with your digestive system, muscles, pancreas and adrenal glands. Your sensitivity, ambition and ability to achieve are stored here. It can be seen as the seat of your emotional life and is associated with feelings of personal power, laughter, joy and anger.

Anahata (see page 70)

The heart chakra is the center of love, harmony, compassion and peace. Many call it the "house of the soul." It is important to keep this chakra in balance so that we can remain in the right emotional state. Heartbreak or emotional abuse can affect not only the heart, but also the lungs, arms, hands and thymus gland, which produces T cells to boost the immune system.

Vishuddha (see page 84)

The throat chakra is symbolized by the color of the sky, either light blue or turquoise. The name, translated from the original Sanskrit, means "purification" or "cleansing." It affects our ability to communicate. In balance, it helps inspire calm, assisting us with right speech, honesty and good decision-making. However, not being able to express ourselves properly can lead to anxiety, a cold, a sore throat or an ear infection.

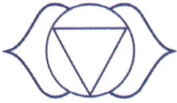

Ajna (see page 96)

Known as the third eye chakra, this is located in the center of the head, slightly above the eyes and between the eyebrows. This is the seat of wisdom and insight, and helps keep things in perspective. Its color is a deep, rich indigo, and it is said to be the link between the higher and the lower self. This chakra is used to question the spiritual nature of our life. It is the chakra of question, perception and knowing. It is concerned with inner vision, intuition and wisdom. It also holds your dreams for this life and recollections of other lifetimes.

Sahasrara (see page 108)

This chakra sits on the top of the head. It is the highest form of chakra, and opens up spiritual communication between the body and the universe, the finite and the infinite. It is said to be the chakra of divine purpose and personal destiny. It is concerned with information, understanding, acceptance and bliss. It is the receiver and giver of energy. Some traditions associate it with the color white, others with violet. It is often represented by a thousand-petaled lotus flower.

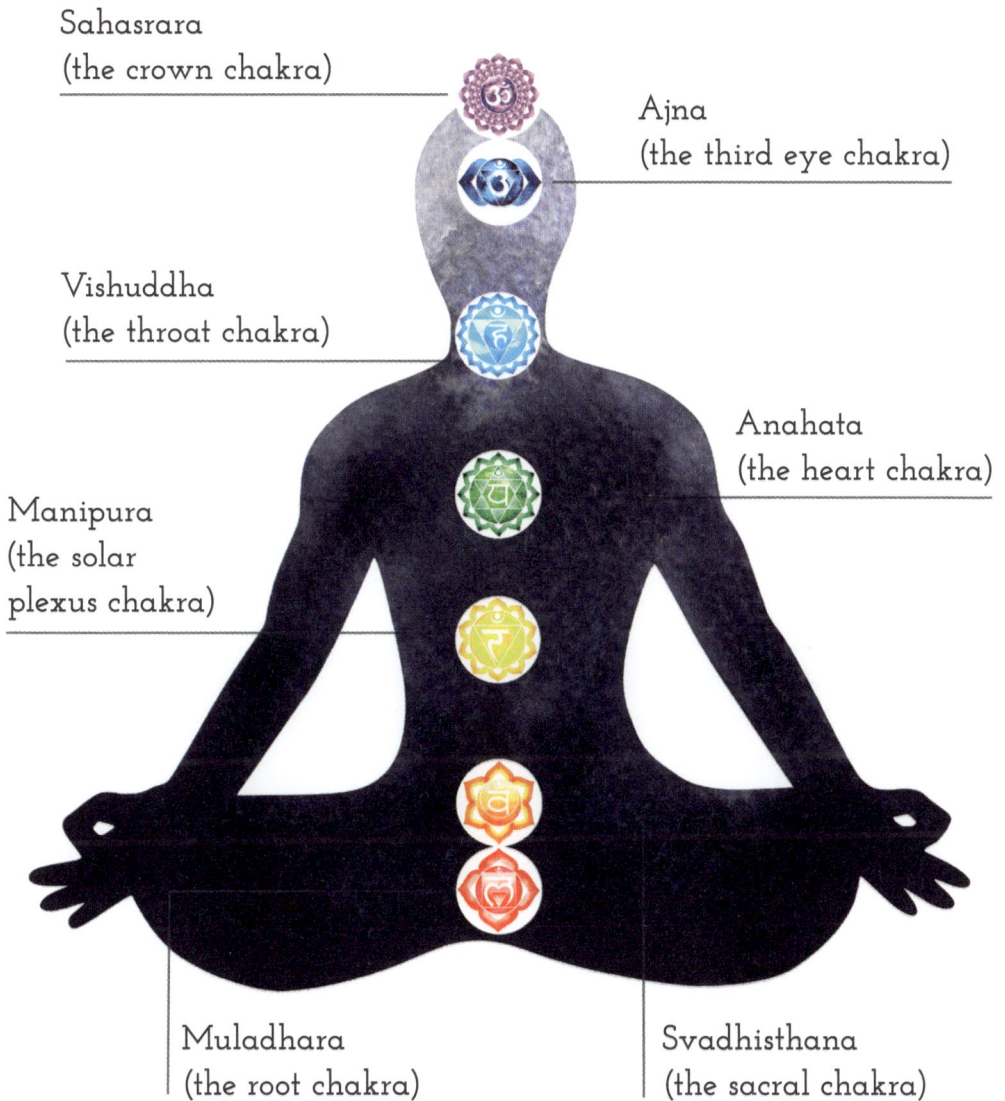

Sahasrara
(the crown chakra)

Ajna
(the third eye chakra)

Vishuddha
(the throat chakra)

Anahata
(the heart chakra)

Manipura
(the solar
plexus chakra)

Muladhara
(the root chakra)

Svadhisthana
(the sacral chakra)

The First Chakra
MULADHARA

COMMON NAME
The root chakra

LOCATION
The perineum, at
the base of the spine
between the anus and
the genitals

ELEMENT
Earth

COLOR
Red

SENSE
Smell

BIJA (SEED) MANTRA
Lam, Om

YANTRA SYMBOL
A four-petaled lotus
with a square inside
and an inverted triangle
inside that

ASSOCIATED DEITIES
Brahma, Ganesha,
Dakini

GEMS AND STONES
Ruby, bloodstone, garnet

Everyone is able to see the beauty of the leaves and flowers of a plant, but few stand in admiration of the roots that lie hidden in the earth below. However, the roots are essential for the survival of any land plant: they anchor it in its place, they absorb water and nutrients from the soil, and they store food. Through this system, the plant gains the strength and the power to penetrate the soil, growing upwards towards the sun to produce flowers, fruit and seeds.

The Muladhara—or root chakra—plays a similar role for human beings. Located at the base of the spine, in the place sometimes known as the pelvic floor, this chakra is responsible for your sense of safety and security. As the focal point of our connection to the earth, situated at the top of our legs and the bottom of our bodies, this is the building block on which our existence is based.

This chakra relates to the element earth and provides the grounding you need in your life; this covers basic needs such as food, water and shelter as well as safety, health, material and emotional needs.

The process starts just after conception; at the center of the soon-to-be fetus is a ball of energy, the *prana,* or "life force," around which the physical body begins to form.

After birth, the right loving care will mean that the child feels secure in the world, trusting that his or her needs will be met. If that care is not given, or is inconsistent, it might manifest itself as chakra blockages in later life.

Electrical connections

With stable foundations and our feet firmly planted, we are connected to the earth through gravity. Being grounded in this way gives us the reassurance we need to find our way in the world. With a stable base, we are able to concentrate our energies in a positive way, without fear. Contact with the earth also provides us with energy as we move through our lives. The Earth is surrounded by an electrostatic field caused by geophysical phenomena such as ionization, ultraviolet radiation from the sun, convection, precipitation and so on. This resonates with micromotions in the body, such as our heartbeat and the movement of bodily fluids, which is helped by the energy that flows up from the earth, though our bodies, and back down through our legs and feet.

Of course, energy is also generated through exercise, and this is an essential tool in balancing the first chakra. So move, walk, run, jump, swim, play football, get a dog, whatever takes your fancy. Do it regularly; make it part of your daily routine. The more exercise you do, the more energy you will generate.

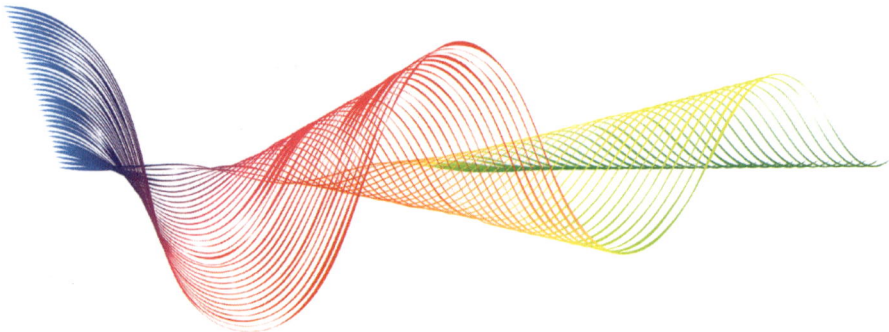

Being grounded helps us feel complete, balanced and stable both bodily and in the mind. Because Muladhara is the first of the bodily chakras, keeping it in balance also creates a solid foundation for the chakras that sit above it.

Body and mind

The body and the mind are in constant interaction during our lives. It is a complex relationship. The Muladhara chakra is the seat of the unconscious. It is here that we hold our flight-or-fight response. It is here that we store or deepest, darkest memories, our hurts, heartbreaks and disappointments. When this chakra becomes active, it can reveal aspects of our characters that we do not necessarily like, such as destructive rage, deep-seated anger or excessive desires. We can also find that we are suffering from an imbalance in the root chakra, which may be mental, such as anxiety or nightmares, or physical, which may manifest itself as a problem in the colon, with the bladder, with elimination, or with pains in the lower back, legs or feet. This begs the question of whether it is better to allow the unconscious to remain buried, rather than stir it up and suffer again.

The answer is not hard to find. It is only by facing the ills of the past that can we let go of our fear in the present. Only when we have faced our weaknesses, regrets and bad decisions can we move forward with purpose. We must learn that we are not only responsible for what we do, but also for what we do not do.

Although it hides our secrets, the Muladhara chakra is also the mother who nourishes and raises us. It is also the seat of our dormant wisdom, the stronghold of our emotional strength and other hidden abilities. If you face up to your regrets and the painful feelings in your consciousness, they are brought to the surface, where they can be healed. Along with the bad memories come good ones, as we remember how we overcame adversity, how much we loved those we have lost, how we have felt joy, harmony and freedom. You can learn from your mistakes through reflection, become conscious of the right thing to do, and find the strength to move forward with the right intentions. In this way, we can remove the yoke of past mistakes and clear our path into the future. Revisiting past disappointments can be a positive process, as it can be a transition, a step in our development.

The yantra and associated deities

Yantras are geometric devices used to facilitate meditation. The use of these images comes from the Tantric traditions of Indian religions and were made popular in the West by the psychologist Carl Jung (1875–1961), who found that drawing and coloring them helped him overcome rational thought and access his unconscious. Each of the chakras has a yantra associated with it, which typically includes geometric shapes, deities and other symbols. As well as meditation, yantras can be used for protection, good fortune and healing.

The Muladhara yantra, which is red, has four lotus petals, inside which is a square. Both are representations of the four points of the compass and the four aspects of conscious-ness: mind, intellect, consciousness and ego. Inside the square are four more symbols: an image of the seed sound (lam—see below), which is said to contain the essence of the chakra; an elephant with seven trunks; a downward-pointing triangle, inside which is a crescent moon; and a phallus with a snake coiled around it. The elephant, associated with the elephant-headed god Ganesha, represents strength, its seven trunks indicating the power needed to support all seven major chakras. The triangle represents Shakti (female) energy, while the phallus, or Shiva lingam, represents male energy. Wrapped around this is a coiled snake; this represents Kundalini (an energy and goddess associated with higher consciousness), which is rooted in the Muladhara chakra. Other deities associated with the first chakra are Brahma, the creator of the universe, and his consort, the goddess Dakini.

The bija (seed) mantra

Mantras have been used as an aid to mediation for thousands of years. They can be chanted out loud or silently in order to find an inward focus. When sounded out loud, the sound should be extended so that each repetition runs into the next, creating a drone sound. The most famous, *om*, is the symbol of the Absolute, and represents the merging of our physical and spiritual bodies. It is sometimes written as "aum," because you should begin with the *ahh* sound in the back of your throat, bringing the sound forward in your mouth to *ooo* and *mmm* with your lips closed. This chant can be used to awaken any or all of your chakras, but each chakra has its own seed mantra too. The seed mantra for the Muladhara chakra is *lam* (pronounced "larm"), the sound of spiritual awakening. It releases tensions, removes blockages and activates its energy. And so the process of awakening the dormant powers within us and raising them into consciousness begins.

Meditation

Meditation is a good way of awakening your chakras. This will help you in many ways, enabling you to recognize when they are in balance as well as identifying imbalances or blockages as they occur. The following meditations, one sitting inside and one standing outside, will start the process of awareness for the first chakra. If you identify a problem, move on to the yoga poses (*asanas*) for help in healing and rebalancing (see pages 124-141).

1   Sit in a comfortable position, either cross-legged on the floor or in a chair. Sit up tall with your spine straight, shoulders relaxed and chest open. Rest your hands on your knees or in your lap with the palms facing up. Relax your face, jaw and stomach. Let your tongue rest on the roof of your mouth, just behind the front teeth. Slightly close your eyes.

2   Breathe slowly, smoothly and deeply in and out through your nose. Breathe deep down into the lowest part of your stomach, all the way down to the perineum. Bring your awareness to the first chakra, located between the tip of the tailbone and the bottom of the pubic bone. Notice any sensations here as you take a few slow, deep breaths in and out.

3   Then inhale and engage your pelvic floor by contracting the muscles between the pubic bone and tailbone and drawing the perineum up towards Muladhara. Keep your focus on feeling the pelvic floor and Muladhara as your breath flows in and your muscles contract. Feel your spine lengthen as your feet and legs push down. If comfortable, hold the breath for a few seconds. Then release your muscles and exhale through the nose. Repeat for 3-5 minutes, working on increasing the contraction of your pelvic floor, if comfortable.

4   Return to a slow, deep breath with awareness of Muladhara without engaging the pelvic floor. Feel any sensations here as you take a few slow, deep breaths in and out, noticing any changes. Breathe deeply into Muladhara for 3-5 minutes.

5   To finish, gently let your eyes blink open, inhale with your palms together in front of your heart, exhale and gently bow. Take a moment or two before moving on with the rest of your day.

Outdoor meditation

1 Go into your yard, or a park. You don't need to be in a beautiful place; all you need is enough room to stand, and a little privacy. Take your shoes and socks off, and find a spot where you can stand on the grass or bare earth.

2 Stand with your feet shoulder-width apart. When you feel your bare feet connect with the earth, allow each of your vertebrae to stack and rest straight and tall. Close your eyes, consciously soften your shoulders down, away from your ears, and allow your arms to relax by your sides. With your knees slightly bent, bring your awareness to the soles of your feet.

3 You may become aware of a subtle interplay of energy between the earth and your skin. Notice the weight of your legs and feet pressing down on the ground, and feel that equal and opposite upward force holding you in place. Feel strong and solid. Feel the power in your core; feel the balance at the base of your spine.

4 Breathe in and out. Smell the earth and the grass and the fresh air.

5 Gradually allow your awareness to travel up along your body, feeling each body part stacking on top of the part below it, supported by your foundation.

6   When you reach the point where your spinal cord meets the base of your skull, imagine the crown of your head being lifted high into the sky, and rest in this equilibrium for a few minutes. Stand tall. Exist.

7   When you are ready, slowly blink your eyes open, take a moment or two, and get on with your day.

The Second Chakra
SVADHISTHANA

COMMON NAME
The sacral chakra

LOCATION
The sacrum, in the center of the body below the navel

ELEMENT
Water

COLOR
Orange

SENSE
Taste

BIJA (SEED) MANTRA
Vam, Om

YANTRA SYMBOL
A six-petaled lotus flower with a circle inside it

ASSOCIATED DEITIES
Indra, Varuna, Vishnu

GEMS AND STONES
Carnelian, fire opal, topaz

The second chakra, Svadhisthana, is located above the pubic bone and below the navel at the front, and two finger-widths above the coccyx at the back. It sits near the Muladhara chakra, to which it is closely related, both being connected to physical stimuli and interaction. But where memories lie dormant in the first chakra, here in the second they can find expression. While the first chakra is concerned with survival, the second seeks pleasure and enjoyment. If we consider ourselves vehicles, then the first chakra is the car itself, and the second chakra is the fuel—the passion that fires up the engine so we can make our dreams come true.

The energy of the sacral chakra allows you to let go ("go with the flow"), to move on, to embrace change and transformation. Translated directly from Sanskrit, Svadhisthana means "the dwelling place of the self," marking the point when children move on from infancy and begin to develop as individuals. During the early teen years, one starts to experience the world through feelings, emotions, pleasure and creativity. For these reasons, the second chakra is often associated with Eric Erikson's second stage of human development.

Your inner child

This chakra governs the flow of creative life-force within us. As humans, it is part of our nature to create. As children in the second stage of development (8 to 14 years), we create in our play, inventing games and characters, coloring, painting, building Lego models and so on. As we get a little older and become immersed in the education system, we are generally expected to conform, to follow the rules and fit in with others. This can mean that we lose our creative energy. During adulthood, we get used to doing what's right, following the latest trends, and sticking to what is acceptable. This does not encourage creativity. Indeed, blockages of this chakra are common in adults. While you might be happy to undertake a difficult task that you've done before, if asked to draw a picture or cook a meal without a recipe, you might be forced out of your comfort zone. This is because you have stopped being creative, or stopped taking risks creatively because somewhere along the way someone told you that you couldn't do it. In order to balance your second chakra energy, you need to take risks and not be afraid of failure.

Play is a great way to do this. A child will spend hours building a Lego tower, a sandcastle or a dollhouse. That same child will then smash their masterpiece and start over as if it was no big deal. Start to play like a child. If your gourmet meal doesn't turn out right, so what? If your potted plant dies in a week, plant another one. And yes, if your work project is a failure, it doesn't mean your career is over. Channel your inner child and, like a child at play, start again. You have an infinite amount of creative energy inside you, so use it.

The second chakra is also the wellspring of other aspects of creativity, the raw creativity and passion that artists draw from. But there is creativity in other things too, such as dancing, singing, cooking and gardening. We do each of these things in our own unique way, and they have a beneficial effect on our physical and spiritual selves.

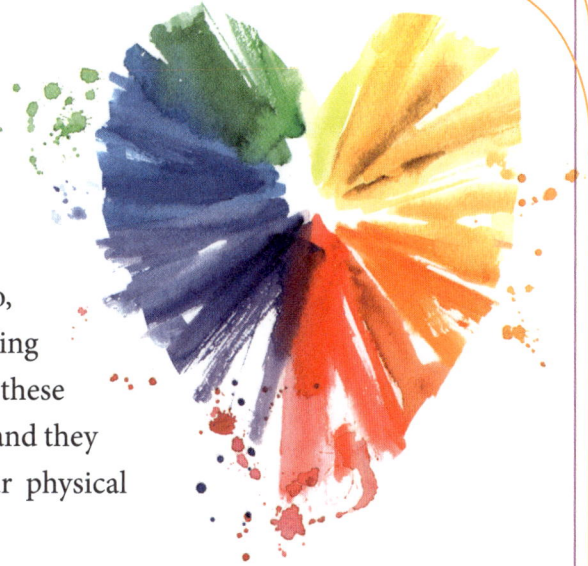

Procreation and the joys of life

Of course, many people express their creativity through procreation, and the second chakra's association with the reproductive glands and organs—a woman's womb is situated in the same location—expresses this beautifully on a physical level. Its energy is feminine, passive and lunar. Naturally, the sacral chakra also has a strong connection to sexuality, which is yet another way of letting your life-force flow, experiencing life in a sensual way.

The second chakra is also the center of pleasure, enjoyment and passion. It allows us to experience life deeply and intensively, as the movement of energy flows through us in the form of sensation, emotion and sensuality. This is one of the strongest forces in us, one that can be difficult to tame. Naturally, it is also considered to be at the root of unconscious desires, as an overflow of passion that can transform into an addiction or obsession. Finding the middle ground between a joyful flow of passion and healthy restriction is the balance that a properly working second chakra maintains.

The sacral chakra is associated with the sense of taste, influencing our sensual experience of the world—really tasting it. It expresses our authentic desire to interact with life in a joyful way, to participate in the creative dance of divine energy, to really feel, enjoy and taste being alive.

Balance/imbalance

The second chakra is concerned with our ability to give and receive love. This helps establish a positive identity at the core level of our being, developing a sense of self-worth. It gives us confidence to offer our friendship to others without condition. A person with a balanced second chakra is trustworthy, intuitive and compassionate. They are grounded, open to the world around them, with an emotional stability and a zest for life. As a consequence, they are always great company.

As we have seen, the main challenge for the health of your second chakra is social conditioning—we live in a society where, by and large, feelings are not valued, and where passion and emotional reactions are frowned upon. We are taught not to "lose control" and, over time, can become disconnected from our bodies and our feelings. This chakra is also under threat from cultural attitudes toward sexuality—on the one hand sexuality is magnified and glorified (for example, in advertising) and on the other hand it is repressed and rejected.

Another challenge comes when we lose sight of our inner child, taking on the adult responsibilities of paying a mortgage, bringing up children and looking after elderly parents. During this period of our lives, there is little space left for pleasure. We can start losing our sense of play, sensuality and sexuality, and start acting like automatons. As a result, we can suppress our sacral chakra, which becomes underactive. As a consequence, we might experience instability, fear of change, sexual dysfunction, depression or addiction.

The yantra and associated deities

The traditional color associated with the Svadhisthana chakra was vermilion. Today it is usually represented as a white lotus with six orange petals. The petals represent six modes of consciousness: *vrittis* (literally "whirlpools," but here it refers to thoughts that swirl through the mind), affection, pitilessness, destructiveness, delusion, disdain and suspicion. Inside the flower there is a circle representing water, the essence of life.

Symbols in the circle include a silver crescent moon, which points toward the close relationship between the phases of the moon and the fluctuations of the tides and of human emotions. For some, this symbolism also relates to the feminine menstrual cycle that takes a

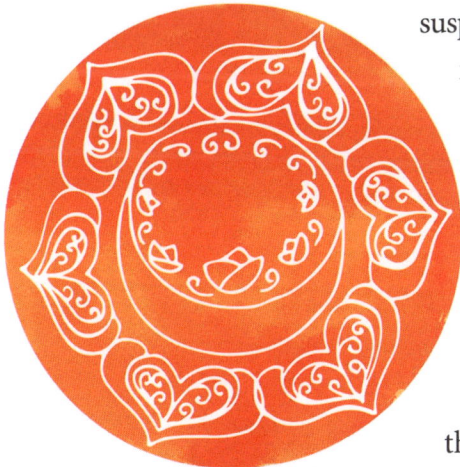

similar number of days as the phases of the moon to complete, although this is not scientifically correct. However, the connection of the sacral chakra with sexual organs and reproduction is represented by a fish-tailed alligator. This mythical creature is said to represent male sexual power; alligator fat was once used to enhance male virility.

In terms of deities, the second chakra is presided over by Vishnu, the all-pervading life-force in the universe; Varuna, god of the cosmic waters; and Indra, god of the heavens, thunder and lightning, storms, rivers and war.

The bija (seed) mantra

The *Upanishads* explain that the five lower chakras are related to the five elements (or *bhutas*) that make up the world: earth (*prithivi*), water (*apas/ jala*), fire (*tejas/agni*), air (*vayu*) and ether (*akasha*). Each element has a bija mantra associated with it; when this mantra is sounded, it resonates in the chakra and purifies the *nadis* (subtle channels of energy). The *nadis* link the higher spiritual aspects of our being with our mind, our emotions and our body. The seed mantra for the Svadhisthana chakra is *vam* (pronounced "varm," "vang" or "fvam"). When spoken, it nourishes and purifies bodily fluids and brings alignment with the waters. To create the right noise, start with your upper teeth on your lower lip, and produce a breathy consonant similar to the sound of a car revving: *fvaarm*. Don't forget that the *om* chant (see pages 43-44) can be used in healing all the seven main chakras.

Meditations

The following two meditations will start the process of awareness for the second chakra. If you identify a problem, move on to the yoga *asanas* (see pages 124-141) for help in healing and rebalancing.

1   Sit in a comfortable meditation pose of your choice. Close your eyes. Breathe gently through both nostrils, with your lips sealed. Imagine you are standing by a shallow lake of still water.

2   Imagine that someone drops a large, shiny pebble into the lake. Watch as the ripples grow outwards and disappear.

3   Allow your breath to become progressively shallower, until it is just coming to the end of your nostrils.

4   As your breath becomes calmer, so will your mind. Make sure your breath doesn't make any ripples on the surface of the lake. As the water grows still again, focus all your attention on seeing the pebble on the bottom of the lake.

5 If other thoughts start to arise in your mind, do not try to drive them away. The more you try, the more they will return. Become indifferent to these thoughts, focusing only on the pebble. The other thoughts will gradually disperse.

6 When the surface of the lake is completely still, you can see to the bottom clearly. When the surface is agitated by ripples or the wind, this is impossible. The same is true of your mind. When it is still, you will experience inner peace.

7 To finish, gently let your eyes blink open, inhale with the palms of your hands over your lower stomach, then exhale gently. Take a moment or two before going on with your day.

✳ ✳ ✳

1 Sit or lie in a comfortable position. Ensure that your spine is straight so that energy can flow freely through it.

2 Become aware of your natural breath—how it enters and leaves your body. Where it is in your body? Is it high in your chest? Is it short or long? Don't change it; just observe it.

3 Bring your attention to the location of this chakra, a couple of inches below your belly button.

4   Deepen your breath as you keep your awareness in this area.

5   Visualize a pool of water inside your pelvis; it is a calm and soft body of water. Keep your awareness there as you breathe. In the body of water is the reflection of a beautiful sunset. The water glows with a beautiful orange hue. Water has the ability to take many forms, from the ocean to the rain, from a flowing river to a deep and still lake. Acknowledge its adaptability. The human body is made mostly of water, and is in constant motion (even as you are sitting in stillness, much is happening on a cellular level). And you are also adaptable.

6   Breathe, and be aware of the beauty of the glowing water of the lake. There are no ripples on the water. It is still, and the reflection of the sunset is clear. Revel in the scene for a few minutes.

7   To finish, gently let your eyes blink open, inhale with your palms together in front of your lower stomach, then gently exhale.

The Third Chakra
MANIPURA

COMMON NAME
The solar plexus chakra

LOCATION
Between the navel
and the bottom of the
sternum

ELEMENT
Fire

COLOR
Yellow

SENSE
Sight

BIJA (SEED) MANTRA
Ram, Om

YANTRA SYMBOL
A 10-petaled lotus
flower with a
downward-pointing
triangle inside it

ASSOCIATED DEITIES
Agni, Vishnu, Lakini

GEMS AND STONES
Topaz, yellow
tourmaline

The third chakra, like the first two, is Earth-based rather than celestial, and deals with what gives us security in our lives. The solar plexus chakra is located above your navel and below your sternum. It functions as the center of energy associated with ego. It's the source of personal power, self-belief and self-worth. Your solar plexus chakra is activated when you muster the courage to do something that scares you, speak up for yourself or exert your willpower and self-control. You'll notice that in these situations, a balanced third chakra will mean your energy level is high, your posture is tall and commanding, and your voice is firm. However, it's important to note that personal power doesn't mean power over others. It means self-mastery—the ability to master your thoughts and emotions, overcome fear, and take appropriate action in any situation.

The Sanskrit word for the solar plexus is *manipura*, which means "shining gem" or "city of jewels." The chakra contains many of these "shining gems" in the form of qualities such as clarity, self-confidence, bliss, knowledge, wisdom and the ability to make correct decisions. This chakra is represented as a vivid golden yellow. Like a ray of sunshine, this chakra lights your path and warms your body with the glow of self-confidence. It is here that we feel our "gut instinct," the feeling that we get when we are sure of the decision we are about to make. This is also where we feel hollow—some call it "butterflies"—when we are about to do something that makes us nervous, like taking a test or making a speech.

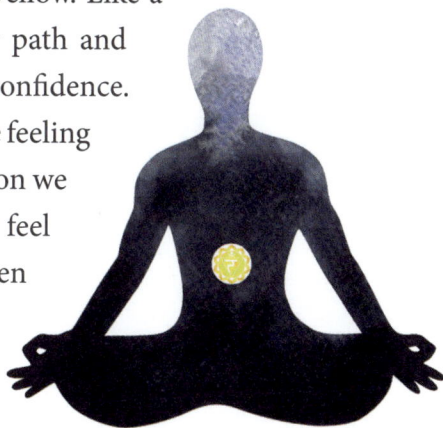

The explorer

This chakra speaks to your creativity, your personality, your intellect and your ego. According to the ancient traditions, its yellow color comes from the "solar" power of the sun and its fire. If it is open and in balance, it will empower you with self-respect and confidence. You will be happy, outgoing, and ready to face new challenges with confidence. This is the chakra of the charismatic leader, the explorer. A key element in developing balance for this chakra is understanding yourself.

As you explore the third chakra, you are searching for your personal power, what you want to be in relation to the external world. It is here that you develop the "self," so that your ego no longer needs the input of others to tell you who you are. For this, you must develop a relationship with yourself. The element of this chakra is fire, and should be used to determine your strength of character. It is with personal power and strength of will that you can conquer the inertia that comes from fear, and move forward through life. The solar plexus chakra can empower you not to be distracted, to follow your true path.

Criticism and rejection

Self-confidence is a fragile thing, and few people can maintain it at all times. Life can sometimes seem full of knocks, put-downs, rejection and disappointments; stress at work or at home can also be debilitating. And it doesn't take much for this chakra to be knocked off balance or even blocked. In fact, criticism and rejection are two of the biggest contributors to a blocked solar plexus chakra. We might start to worry about what others think of us. This can quickly erode self-worth, leading to pessimism and low expectations. A persistent lack of self-confidence can cause people to see themselves as victims, so that they put up with poor treatment, eroding their resolve to do anything and eventually leading to inertia. Low energy levels, a lack of willpower, and feeling cold emotionally and physically are also indicators of Manipura deficiency.

A closed third chakra can manifest itself as physiological problems too. Due to the location of this chakra in the center of the body, digestive problems such as indigestion, nausea, ulcers, diabetes, anorexia, celiac disease and liver disease are associated with a blocked solar plexus chakra.

Getting the balance right

However, balance means that even with self-esteem, calm and initiative, this chakra also requires respect for others. People with a healthy solar plexus chakra do not brag about their accomplishments—they let their results speak for themselves. They are confident but kind. People who have excessive energy flow to the third chakra are usually overly aggressive.

They can be dominating, controlling, manipulative and power-hungry. These people are very competitive. Those with feelings of inadequacy will dramatically overcompensate. This false show of bravado and self-glorification may be seen as confidence or arrogance, but it is false, and crumbles easily. This can lead to serious depression and further over-compensatory behavior. Others are shy and, though they are not prepared to take on a leadership role themselves, are always quick to criticize others. They are also prepared to fail and blame others for their failure.

The key to a healthy solar plexus chakra is finding a balance between being heard without overpowering others with false displays of confidence.

Feel the fear and do it anyway

The fact is, bad things happen. The important thing is how we deal with them. Do we sink? Do we carry on in an unhealthy relationship? Do we continue to do a job that doesn't use our skills? Does the fear of aging, balding, obesity or criticism stop us from living our lives? Or do we swim? Do we move forward? Do we find the courage to take risks? Do we "feel the fear and do it anyway"? A healthy, balanced third chakra will show us the way forward.

As we have discussed, lack of self-confidence (perhaps consistent in certain areas of your life, following a traumatic incident, or even simply after suffering one of life's regular setbacks) is a common issue that most of us face regularly. Inertia might be a short-term issue for you. Why not try one or more of the following things to get yourself going? Start slowly and build up:

* Do exercises designed to strengthen your core: crunches, sit-ups, the mountain climber, the plank, and leg lifts

* Dance

* Practice yoga

* Eat yellow foods such as bananas, corn, and grains (see page 144)

* Drink herbal teas

* Wear yellow and introduce yellow accents into your home environment

* Encourage yourself to step out of your comfort zone by changing your daily routine

* Seek out new experiences and unexplored wisdom to expand your repertoire of knowledge and skills

Take chances, and take yourself out of your comfort zone. Your natural confidence will begin to re-emerge. It might be a little scary at first, but it focuses us to be in the moment and stop overthinking. Let your actions speak for themselves, and find the courage to act by focusing on your strengths and taking small, proactive steps.

The yantra and associated deities

The use of yantras as an aid to meditation is widespread. They are said to be symbolic representations of divine or cosmic forces, a window into the Absolute. When the mind is concentrated on a single, simple object, it helps clear mental chatter, allowing it to remain empty and silent and to permit contemplation of higher thoughts. The ten shining yellow lotus petals of this yantra correspond to the *vrittis* (whirlpools of thought) of jealousy, spiritual ignorance, thirst, treachery, fear, shame, disgust, foolishness, delusion and sadness, and the ten *pranas*, the vital forces that control and nourish the functions of the human body. They also refer to our ability to manipulate our surroundings, often via the ten fingers on our hands. Inside the circle of petals is a fiery-red downward-pointing triangle, which indicates the spread of energy, growth and development. Inside the triangle is the symbol of the seed mantra. It also has three T-shaped projections (called *svastikas*) indicating movement. Below the triangle is a ram, a powerful and energetic animal representing the strength and power of who we are in the world. The deities associated with this chakra are Agni, the god of fire; Vishnu, symbolic of human consciousness; and his partner Lakini, who is able to dispel fear and grant boons.

The bija (seed) mantra

A mantra works in a similar way to a tuning fork. As the tuning fork rings out a note, it vibrates. And, as we use our vocal cords to make certain sounds, they too vibrate. These vibrations channel cosmic energy through our bodies, which generate healing powers. The aim of these seed mantras is to help us get onto the frequency that relates to each particular chakra. The seed mantra for the third chakra is *ram*, pronounced "rang." The "r" is produced with the tip of the tongue curling up to the roof of your mouth. When you get the sound right, you will feel the mantra resonating from the navel. The sound is said to assist longevity. If you find the mantras useful for you, don't forget that the *om* chant (Pages 43-44) is an effective healing method for all seven of the main chakras, so try using both during your meditation sessions.

Meditations

1   Choose a quiet place in your yard or the park. Stand tall, ideally in the sun, and close your eyes.

2   With your arms by your sides, take a few moments to turn your attention inward. When your breathing is steady and unhurried, notice the ground beneath your feet and the space above your head.

3   Breathing in, slowly draw your arms up to the sky; visualize a bright yellow flame igniting in the core of your abdomen. As you exhale, lower your arms in one fluid motion.

4   Continue this flow, feeling the chakra color grow bigger and more vibrant with every inhalation. As you connect with the Earth beneath you and the astral world above you, feel the perfect equilibrium in which you exist.

5   When the shining yellow light has engulfed your entire body, keep your arms overhead and breathe, embracing a strong sense of your personal power and dosing yourself generously with healthy self-esteem.

6   When you are ready, slowly blink your eyes open. Give yourself a moment and then go on with the rest of your day.

* * *

1   Light a candle or tealight (or two) if you are indoors, especially if it is dark.

2   Sit down in a comfortable position for meditation.

3   Cup your left hand and make a fist with your right hand, extending your right thumb up. Place your right fist in your left palm, and draw your hands in front of your solar plexus (just below the sternum and above the navel). Close your eyes. Connect to the rise and fall of your breath.

4   Imagine that your right thumb is a flame flickering at the center of your being. With each inhalation, watch the yellow flame grow a little bit brighter. Imagine a warmth spreading from this area of your body and filling you from the inside out.

5   Now, imagine that you have gathered a little stack of sticks. On each stick, write a word or phrase representing something in your life that is no longer serving you, something that you are in the process of letting go, or need to be. Remember that some things must be let go of hundreds of times before we are free of them. Forgive yourself during this process, because letting go is one of the hardest things to do.

6   Now, place each stick into your flame. Watch it catch fire. And burn. And as each stick is completely burned, imagine that a gust of wind travels into your hands and carries the ash away from you—far, far away.

7   Ask yourself: Do I have the energy to do the things I want to do? Do I have the confidence to do the things I want to do? What gets in the way? Often, our energy is drained in one area of our life, and we are left lifeless for the mountain of wonderful, enriching experiences that could be.
    Breathe.

8   Connect to the rise and fall of your breath. When you are ready, blink your eyes open, and take a moment before going back to your day.

The Fourth Chakra
ANAHATA

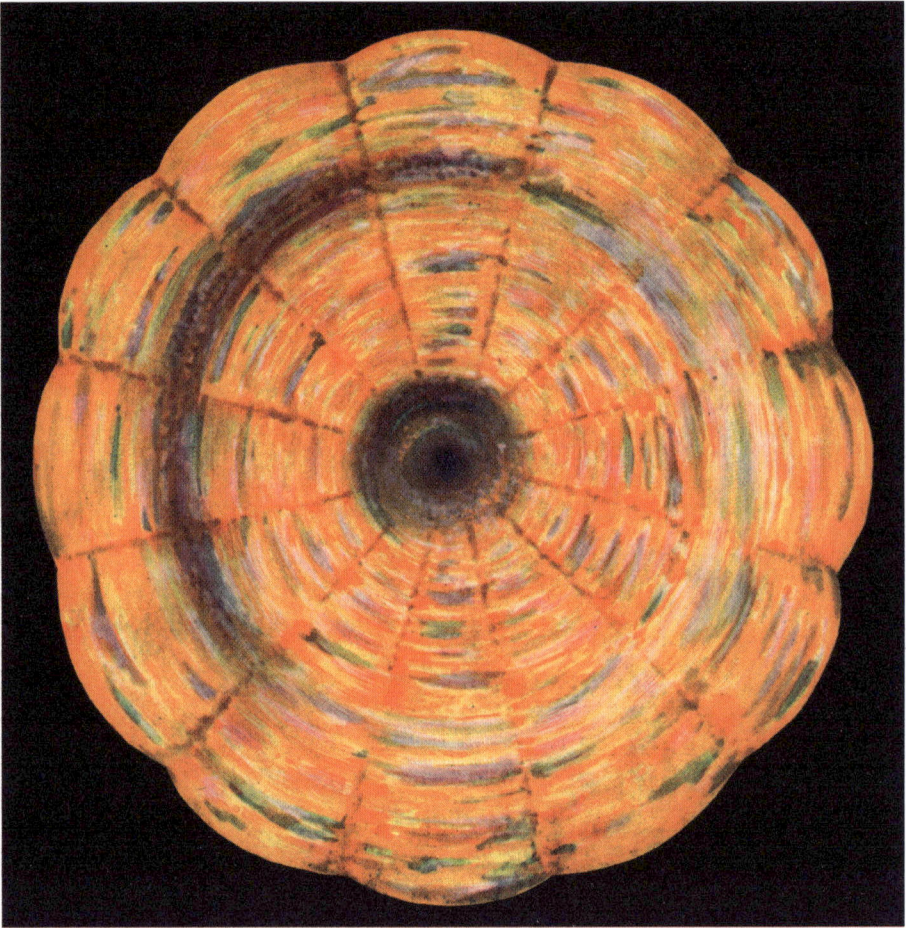

COMMON NAME
The heart chakra

LOCATION
The cardiac plexus,
including the heart,
lungs and thymus gland

ELEMENT
Air

COLOR
Green

SENSE
Touch

BIJA (SEED) MANTRA
Lam, Om

YANTRA SYMBOL
A circle of 12 lotus
petals, inside which is a
six-pointed star

ASSOCIATED DEITIES
Rudra, Vayu, Kakini

GEMS AND STONES
Emerald, jade, peridot,
rose quartz

The heart sits at the center of our bodies. It pumps out our life blood and beats out the rhythm of our lives. It is also the seat of love, the greatest power we have on the Earth. It is through love that we really live; it is through love that we build relationships that make us whole. Without the heart, there is no health, no healing. Without the heart and its love, life is meaningless and we wither and die. Everything begins and ends with love. Love is free, abundant and limitless. Anahata, the central chakra, unifies the physical chakras below and those of the spirit above. As a consequence, it is the most important chakra of all.

The heart chakra is the wheel of energy located at the level of the sternum, or breastbone. It encompasses the heart, lungs, sternum, clavicle, shoulder blades, breast tissue, thymus gland and rib cage. The arms and hands are also extensions of this chakra. The heart is made of a unique type of muscle tissue called cardiac muscle. This allows the heart to beat without getting tired. Cardiac muscle has a higher percentage of mitochondria—the power sources of the cells—than skeletal muscle, so it does not fatigue.

But this tireless service cannot happen unless the heart itself is nourished. When oxygen-rich blood leaves the heart, it travels through the aorta and out into the body. The first branch off of the aorta is back to the muscles of the heart itself. The first thing the heart does is nourish itself. It serves the entire body every day, for our whole life, but it will always take care of its own needs first.

Love and judgment

When we think of love, it is easy to be trite. Perhaps we think about innocent babies, puppies or kittens. Perhaps we imagine kids with big eyes or stock phrases like "love means never having to say you're sorry." We might also think of steamy sex that we've already had or are looking forward to. But these concepts are not really sustainable. Babies and puppies grow; and statistically, the "in love" feeling of a romantic relationship lasts about two years, and is part of our primeval need to make sure the human race continues.

The heart has more spiritual concerns. Just as it nourishes itself first, it allows us to love ourselves first, then to love others, to let others love us, and to give and receive love from all of humanity. What the heart really wants is unconditional love, and that is a challenge; the challenge to sustain this feeling through the grind of daily life after those initial two years, to love those we judge, and to love ourselves. It is only when you have love and compassion for yourself that you can truly love others in a healthy, happy and healing way.

The heart's message is that you can't really help others unless you help yourself. If we judge and condemn our frailties and our faults, as we do those of others, we will find it hard

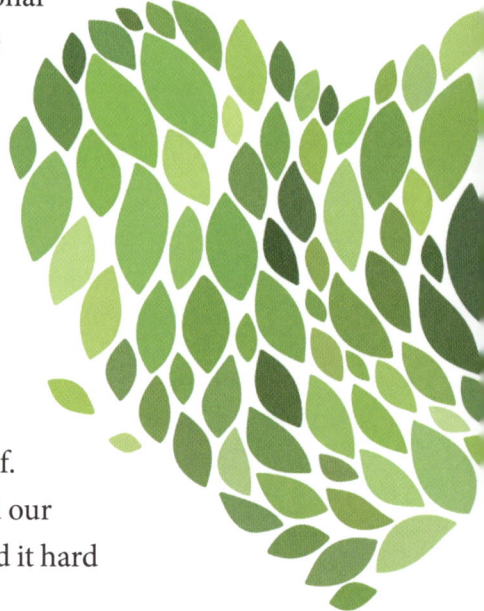

to love. If a mother dedicates herself wholly to her child, and takes no rest or nourishment for herself, then both she and the child will suffer. If a doctor spends too much time with patients and not enough on rest, then mistakes might result. A balanced heart chakra must begin with self-care.

Compassion and forgiveness

As we journey through the vicissitudes of our emotional lives, we should seek balance. When the heart chakra is balanced, it allows us to experience feelings of compassion, selflessness and healing. The world revolves around ourselves and our feelings. Compassion helps us realize that we are not the only ones suffering; it reminds us that we are all in the same boat. This unifies us, connecting us with the whole of humanity. If the heart is too weak, we lack trust and disconnect from others. If it is too open, we can easily be overwhelmed by sympathy for others. Overattachment can make us desperate for connections; a need for detachment might make us push people away rather than risk being vulnerable. The solution is to recognize our own human-ness, to accept our faults and failings as well as those of others, and to trust that the need for love and compassion will be met.

In terms of romantic love and friendship, it is impossible to avoid situations where someone might hurt you. When you get hurt, you have several choices. You can live in a place of grievance, unable to forgive. You can hold on to bad feelings, and develop anger, bitterness and resentment. As well as depression, physical afflictions caused by the blockage in the fourth chakra can include cardiac

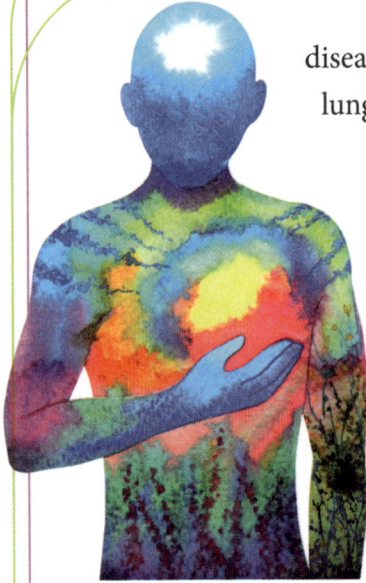

disease, arrhythmia, pneumonia, asthma, allergies and lung conditions. Or you can look that pain in the face, feel it, and then let it go. Your mind and your ego might tell you otherwise, but it really is as simple as that.

The Sanskrit name for the heart chakra, Anahata, means "unhurt", "unstruck" or "unbeaten." Symbolically, this means that beneath the hurts and grievances of past experiences lies a pure and spiritual place where no hurt exists.

The yantra and associated deities

The anahata yantra features a lotus flower with 12 lustrous green petals, which match the divine qualities of the heart. In the center are two overlapping, intersecting triangles, making a shape known as a *shatkona* that resembles the Star of David. The six points of the star are said to represent the other six chakras. The triangle facing upwards symbolizes Shiva, the male principle, matter rising to meet spirit. The other triangle, facing downward, symbolizes Shakti, the female principle, as spirit descends to inhabit the body. A balance is attained when these two forces are joined in harmony; this is the source of all creation. Inside the central part of the shatkona is the symbol for the seed mantra *yam*, and a golden triangle indicating the divine light that can be revealed when the chakra is fully opened. Inside that, a crescent moon lights the path to enlightenment and shows the psychic blocks that must be dissolved to achieve it. The chakra's associated animal is the black antelope or gazelle, symbolizing the lightness, speed and freedom of the fourth chakra's element, air. The goddess presiding over this chakra is Kakini, who synchronizes the beat of our hearts with the beat of the cosmos. The presiding deity is Rudra, the manifestation of Shiva, while seed mantra yam (see below) is believed to be the sound form of Vayu, lord of the wind.

The bija (seed) mantra

The name mantra is taken from the Sanskrit words *man*, meaning "to think" and *tra*, meaning "liberate." The use of mantras to aid meditation was adopted by Hatha yoga practitioners for use in keeping focus during their sessions. They particularly helpful in keeping your mind focused on your breath. Chanting a mantra during your practice can help reduce *chitta vritti*, or mind chatter. The seed mantra for the heart chakra is *yam* (pronounced "yarm" or "yang"). Anahata is the center of the seven main chakras, where the physical body and the spiritual body meet. Therefore, it affects both physical and spiritual well-being. The mantra gives control over the breath and is said to promote love, compassion and forgiveness. Always remember that you can prolong your mantra session by chanting *om*, the most sacred syllable symbol and mantra of Brahman, the Almighty God in Hinduism, creator of all existence.

Meditations

1 Sit in a comfortable position, either cross-legged on the floor or in a chair. Sit up tall with your spine straight, your shoulders relaxed and your chest open. Hold your palms together and lightly press the knuckles of the thumbs into the sternum at the level of your heart (you should feel a little notch where the knuckles magically fit). Breathe slowly, smoothly and deeply into your stomach and chest. Lightly close your eyes.

2 Let go of any thoughts or distractions and let your mind focus on feeling the breath moving in and out of your body. Once your mind feels quiet and still, bring your focus to the light pressure of the thumbs pressing against your chest and feel the beating of your heart. Keep this focus for a few minutes.

3 Gently release your hands and rub the palms together, making them warm and energized. Place your right palm in the center of your chest and your left hand on top of your right. Close your eyes and feel the center of your chest warm and radiant, full of energy. See this energy as an emerald-green light, radiating out from the center of your heart into the rest of your body. Feel this energy flowing out into your arms and hands, and flowing back into the

heart. Stay with this visualization for a few minutes.

4   When you feel completely soaked with heart chakra energy, gently release your palms and turn them outwards with the elbows bent, the shoulders relaxed and the chest open. Feel or visualize the green light love energy flowing out of your palms and into the world. You can direct it toward specific loved ones in your life or to all sentient beings.

5   To end your meditation, inhale as you push your arms up toward the sky, connecting with the heavens. Then exhale and lower the palms lightly to the floor, connecting with the earth. Take a moment or two before moving on with the rest of your day.

✻ ✻ ✻

1   Sit down in a comfortable position. Soften and then close your eyes and allow your mind to relax. Sit tall with your spine and neck long and your shoulders relaxed. Begin to focus on your breath. As you inhale and exhale, focus on different parts of your body and release any tension you feel there.

2   Let go of your thoughts for a moment; feel yourself deeply relaxed. Then focus your attention on your heart. Think of it as a space, and feel the breath enter and leave that space. Feel your heart safe, secure and relaxed.

3 Your heart is a point of awareness, the point where feelings enter. Feel whatever is in there. It might be peace, it might be light, or you might feel stress, disappointment or longing. Don't strain to find anything, just feel whatever is in there; allow it to just be.

4 Keeping your attention there, breathe gently; sense the breath flowing through your heart. Visualize a soft, pastel light or coolness pervading the chest. Now imagine that with each nurturing and nourishing breath, you're wiping away dirt or dust that's covering your heart. Imagine that your breath is actually inhaling into the heart and exhaling out of the heart. Be here, with this breath, for several moments.

5 As you breathe, ask your heart if it wants to say something. For the next few minutes, sit and listen for an answer. It may stay silent and at peace, but it may release emotions, memories, fears and dreams long stored inside. This may release strong emotions, a quickness of breath, or even tears. Whatever happens, let the experience be what it is. If you drift off to sleep or daydream, don't worry. Just bring your attention back to your heart.

6 When you're ready, open your eyes and bring your palms together at your heart center. Bow to your heart, and tell it you'll be with it again soon. Thank it for its loving wisdom and daily guidance.

The Fifth Chakra
VISHUDDHA

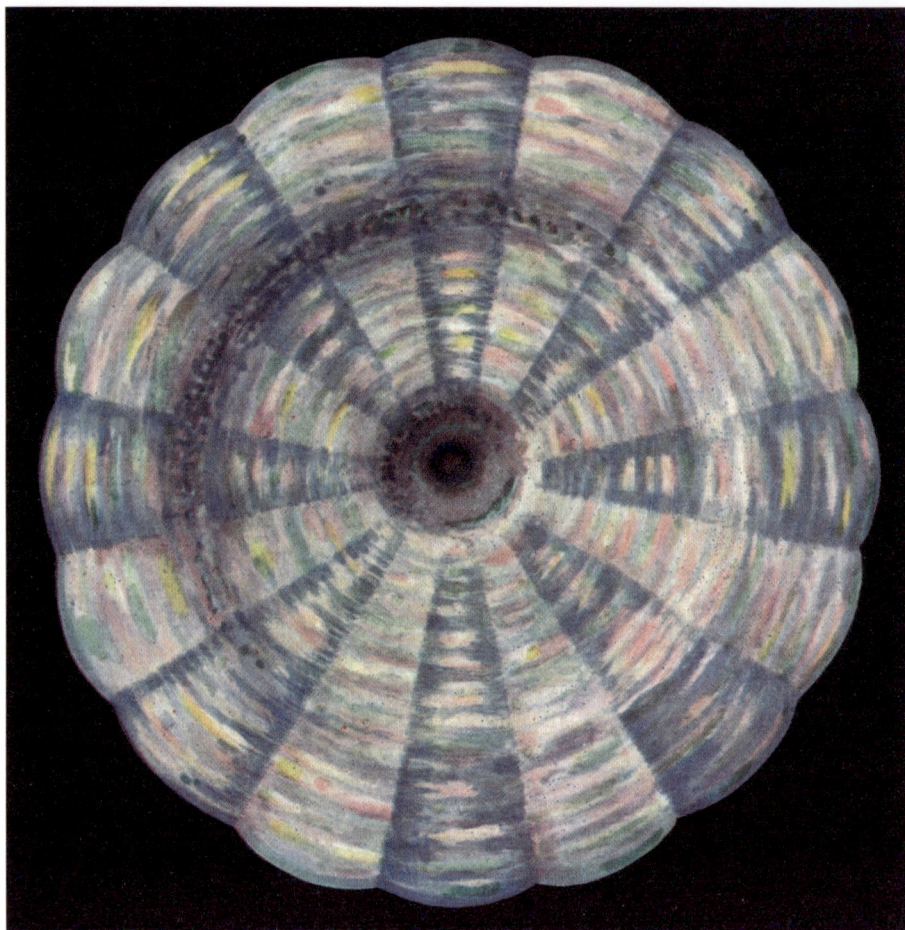

COMMON NAME
The throat chakra

LOCATION
The throat, thyroid,
parathyroid, jaw, neck,
mouth, tongue and
larynx

ELEMENTS
Sound/space/ether

COLOR
Bright blue

SENSE
Hearing

BIJA (SEED) MANTRA
Ham, Om

YANTRA SYMBOL
A circle of 16 lotus
petals, inside which is
a downward-pointing
triangle

ASSOCIATED DEITIES
Ganga, Sarasvati

GEMS AND STONES
Sapphire, blue topaz,
aquamarine, lapis lazuli

The fifth chakra, Vishuddha, is the chakra of communication. Human communication in terms of languages, words and sentences is something that distinguishes us from other species. This use of language is a gift, but one that can be used to heal and harm. Having a voice allows us to express ourselves to our family, to our friends, to everyone. It gives us self-expression, the right to speak and be heard, a voice in the world. It allows to say what is in our heart and soul. It makes us who we are. With communication comes sound, the primary element of this chakra.

The word vishuddha is Sanskrit for "purification" or "pure wisdom," and a major challenge of this energy center is finding the wisdom to determine how to communicate in ways that do justice to you, to others and to any higher consciousness or higher being. In consequence, this is the first of the three spiritual chakras. It sits at the center of the neck, and forms the passage between the body and the head. It is said to be the bridge between our hearts and our minds, our bodies and our spirits.

When blocked, this chakra can make you tongue-tied and unable to express your feelings. You may find that your ability to attract what you want is hampered by an inability to use the right words at the right time. When functioning well, you are able to maintain a strong, balanced relationship with those around you and with the higher realms. Mantras are often used in order to ensure that this chakra is operating to the best of its ability.

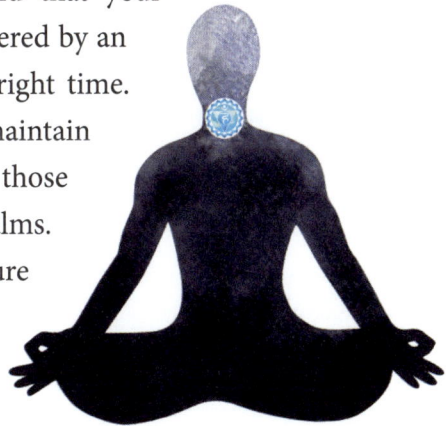

Speaking and listening

Communication involves both speaking and listening. The major life forces of this chakra are sound, vibration and resonance. In order to verbalize our ideas, we must pay attention to how we say the words. Your voice is not merely words, but how you say them. Babies and dogs don't understand the words you say, but through the rhythm and resonance of the sound, they will understand the message. Our voices resonate with the sound of the language we use, so if we speak in a clear and inviting way, others will pick up the rhythm, hearing that and hearing what we actually say.

Of course, it's not always that easy. Authentic expression is not something that comes easily. There's a delicate dance between saying what you mean and being tactful. It's often easier to say what you think the other person may want to hear instead of speaking the truth. Fear of not being accepted, or judgment from others, may hinder your truthful verbal expression.

Listening is another aspect of the fifth chakra. The highest form of listening does not mean shutting up and thinking about the next point you are going to make, while pretending to listen when the other person is talking. It means giving the other person your full attention and really hearing what they say. This might mean putting away your cell phone or turning off your computer, and waiting to hear the other person completely before responding.

Telling the truth

Work on the lower chakras will help prepare you for this. When you align the first and second chakras, it helps with overcoming fear. Opening the third chakra helps you feel your personal power and have the confidence to express yourself. Knowing what's in your heart comes when you align the fourth chakra. Then, when it comes to verbalizing your needs, desires and opinions, you're better able to determine how to be truthful to yourself and others. It is to this process that the word *vishuddha*, "purifier," refers.

Dr David Simon, a world-renowned authority in the field of mind-body medicine, often quoted the following ancient wisdom. He said that there are three gateways you should cross before speaking:

* First, ask yourself, "Is what I am about to say true?"

* If so, proceed to the second gateway and ask, "Is what I am about to say necessary?"

* If the answer is yes, go to the third gateway and ask yourself, "Is what I am about to say kind?"

Speaking your highest truth doesn't mean you're allowed to be hurtful or critical. The truth from your spiritual essence will come across as kind and compassionate.

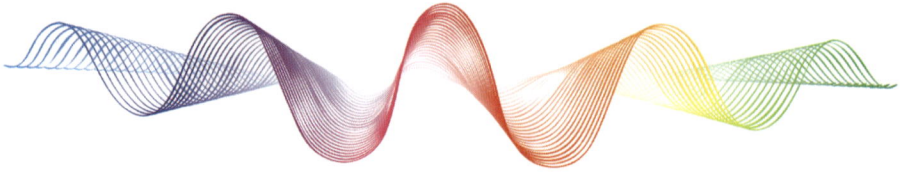

Between the heart and the head

In *The Descent of Man* (1871), Charles Darwin had a theory that human voices developed when chest and throat muscles contracted in excitement or fear, suggesting that voice and emotion come from the same impulse. Might this be why a lump in the throat is often the first sign of emotional distress? When someone feels anxiety or tension, their speaking voice is affected. Of course, the opposite is true. Your mood can be lifted by chanting and through yoga poses, for example, and many people swear by the restorative effects of singing, particularly singing in a choir. Biologists tell us that this is because of breathing, the release of endorphins, and because singing gets more oxygen into the blood.

But there is more to it than that. Singing touches something deep inside us. Why is it that all spiritual practices sing hymns or mantras? They are used to clear the mind and help us unite with a divine entity. Ann Dyer, a yoga instructor and singer, explains: "The voice lies between the heart and the head. So, on a very basic level, the act of chanting brings together your intellectual awareness with your heart awareness." This idea is backed up by another singing yogi, Suzanne Sterling, who explains that, "At the molecular level, we are vibrating entities," and because the voice is a vibration it communicates directly with our core. When we allow certain tones to run through our bodies, it can bring us back to harmony.

Western medicine is catching on to this idea too, and listening to music is recognized as a part of therapy, and pain and stress management. Studies carried out during the last thirty years have proved that singing can have both physical and psychological benefits. Ann Dyer recommends yoga and daily chanting. "The more familiar your voice becomes to you," she says, "the more it will begin to reveal your truest self." Your state of being is reflected in your voice, or as she calls it, "the barometer of your being."

A healthy and well-balanced fifth chakra will enable you to express yourself, though your voice, in a manner that is nurturing both for yourself and for others. Those who speak too softly may be unable to speak their truth, or may be oppressed in some way. Those who shout are clearly not listening to others, and their conversations are most likely to be rather short. They would do well to take notice of the saying that "in order to be a great conversationalist, try listening." There are many symptoms of an unbalanced Vishuddha chakra, including a stiff neck, sore throat, blocked ears, swollen glands and laryngitis.

Yantra and associated deities

The yantra symbol for Vishuddha is a sixteen-petaled lotus around a white circle, thought to represent the full moon or the element ether. On each petal is a letter from the Sanskrit alphabet through which communication is possible. Inside this circle is a silver crescent, the symbol of the cosmic sound *nadam* (the "inner music" we hear when we stop chanting),

indicating purity in the sound of silence. There is also a downward-pointing triangle, *akasa mandala*, which represents Shakti, the female power of creation. Inside the triangle is the symbol for the seed mantra *ham*. Below them is the elephant with seven trunks, Alravata, also present in the Muladhara yantra, who serves all the major chakras with his strength and power. The deity that governs the fifth chakra is Sarasvati, the goddess of flow, speech, knowledge and the arts, while Ganga (named after the river Ganges), symbolizes the purification of sins granted to those who bathe in its waters every day.

The bija (seed) mantra

Mantras, particularly single-syllable bija mantras, are usually chanted for their healing sound vibrations rather than any specific meaning. They are thought to clear the subtle energy pathways in the body in order to create positive change. Chant the bija mantras either one at a time or in sequence. Used in sequence with the chakras, they will resonate up and down the spine. The first sound (consonant) should be shorter than the second, and the final sound, usually "m" or "n" should be held for longer. Repetition can help you access a meditative state. The bija mantra for the vishuddha chakra is *ham* (pronounced "hum" or "hang"). The "h" sound is produced at the back of the throat. This chant is said to energize the throat and the brain, bringing sweetness and harmony to your voice. If chanting is helpful to you, you can extend the session by using the *om* chant (see pages 43-44), which is helpful in opening all of your chakras. The two chants can even be sung together, as in "aumhum."

Meditation

1   Sit down in a comfortable position. Shut your eyes and take a long, deep breath. As you exhale, move your attention to your throat and imagine a sapphire-blue chakra. The blue glow of the chakra spreads like a vibration or a pulse from your throat to fill your neck and head first, and then the rest of your body.

2   Imagine walking through a forest on a narrow path that is lined on both sides by huge shade trees. You hear the sounds insects, small animals scurrying around, and chirping birds. In the distance, a stream flowing over its rocky bed makes a pleasant gurgling sound.

3   You find a small clearing in which a giant log has fallen on the forest floor. You walk up to it and sit with your back resting against the log.

4   The sounds of the forest become even more evident to you. There is a magical quality to them, and you can now hear the faintest of sounds. The whole forest is playing a symphony, especially for you.

5   Now see your fifth chakra spinning and gaining strength. As it spins faster, a blue light washes over you and pervades every cell, every pore in your body.

6 Breathe deeply and feel the energy funneling into your throat, which is bursting with dazzling blue light. Rest in this awareness.

7 Gently stand up and start walking back from the clearing to the edge of the forest, where you first started. Look back at the singing forest and feel at one with it.

8 When you are ready, open your eyes, stand up and move on with the rest of your day.

Second throat meditation

1 Sit in a chair with your feet flat on the floor, or on a cushion or pillow, wherever you feel comfortable. Slowly blink your eyes closed. Bring your awareness to your breath. Notice the rise and fall of your chest, the natural rhythm of your breathing. Sit and breathe for a few moments.

2 If you find your thoughts wandering, let them. Welcome the thoughts, then gently let them go by coming back to this meditation. Now, make two or three deep yawns. You can "fake yawn" until a real one comes along. Then bring your attention back to the breath. Notice the natural rhythm of your breathing.

3   At the base of the throat is your throat chakra. Imagine that it is a tiny sky-blue light, spinning. With each breath, grow this blue light. Expand it first to your neck. Then expand it again to the mouth, then the ears, then your entire head.

4   Take another breath and continue to expand this light. Expand it until it is all around you and you are in a bubble of blue light. Hold that light all around you for three breaths. Focus this beautiful blue light back on the throat. Coat the throat with the light, both inside and out. Illuminate the voice box, the thyroid and all around the neck. Send this light to your mouth to coat your teeth, tongue and lips. This light expands to your ears, awakening your ability to listen. This light heals all these areas as it moves over them. Breathe in the light.

5   Keep your eyes closed or hooded as you near the end of this meditation. It's important to come out of meditation slowly. Bring your awareness back to the breath. Allow yourself to feel the in-and-out rhythm of the rise and fall of the breath.

6   On your next inhalation, wiggle your fingers and toes. Gently shift your arms or legs as needed.

7   When you're ready, open your eyes with a soft downward gaze. Keep your focus inward. Open your eyes fully when you're ready.

The Sixth Chakra
AJNA

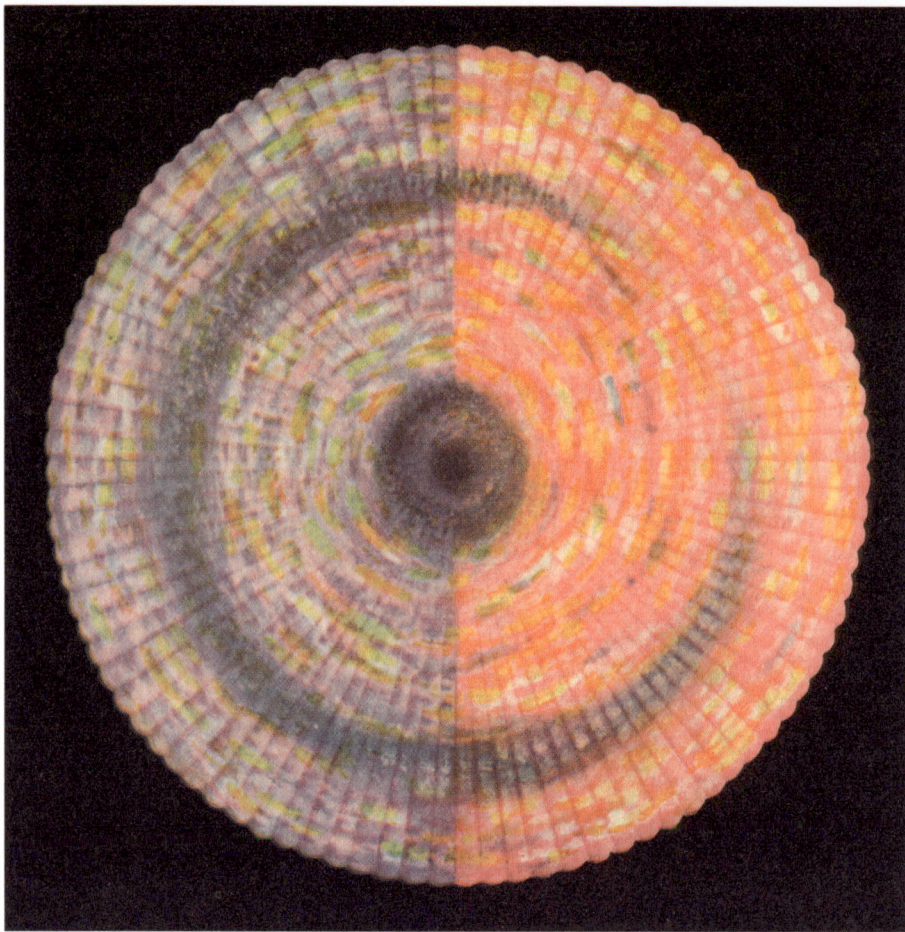

COMMON NAME
The brow or third-eye chakra

LOCATION
The center of the head, between and slightly above the level of the eyebrows

ELEMENT
Light

COLOR
Deep blue/indigo

SENSE
Sight

BIJA (SEED) MANTRA
Om

YANTRA SYMBOL
Two white lotus petals around a circle, inside which is a downward-pointing triangle

ASSOCIATED DEITIES
Shiva, Hakini Shakti

GEMS AND STONES
Diamonds, emeralds, sapphire

The sixth chakra is located in the area of the third eye, which is found in the space between and slightly above the eyebrows. It encompasses the pituitary gland, the eyes, the head and the lower part of the brain. An invisible yet powerful third eye, this is your center of intuition, often known as the "seat of the soul." It is a metaphorical eye, often marked on a Hindu's forehead with a red dot. Ajna, which in Sanskrit means "beyond wisdom," is a spiritual chakra and, if you let it, it will lead you to inner knowledge.

A current theme in spiritual teaching is that the world is an illusion, and that you must search through the dogma—from our culture, politics and social structures—to arrive at your own personal truth. But this is easier said than done. After all, we can all see solutions to others' problems more easily than we can see our own. Our left brain also does a great job of hiding inner truth from our consciousness. How often do you find yourself thinking, "Oh, that can't possibly happen," moments before it does? We have an innate ability to rationalize everything so that we can stay in our comfort zones and continue to believe in our illusions, even though they are often based on fear. Deep inside us all, we hope there is a better and higher way of being. One without fear of making mistakes or doing wrong, and instead filled with joy and happiness. What we must do to find this is take notice of the truths we see through our third eye, the chakra of wisdom and intuition.

Your "sixth sense"

Even before birth, a baby starts to experience the world through its physical senses: hearing its mother's heartbeat, listening to muffled sounds, tasting, touching, and even seeing degrees of light. By the time you are born, you have already learned to trust these senses. While they are essential tools for life in the physical world, they are of little use in a person's spiritual life.

While your physical eyes see things through the reflection of light (without light, the physical eye does not see at all), your third eye "sees" beyond the physical, going into the world of imagination, visualization and clairvoyance. The third eye sees using a different kind of light, the shining light of spiritual insight.

Before the advent of modern technology, intuition was an essential tool. Humans had more reasons to rely on their primal instincts and signals from the environment to guide them. Just like birds are said to know when an earthquake is about to occur, and cats know when it's time for dinner even though they can't read a clock, so humans have an intuitive "sixth sense." We've all heard stories of people

having hunches that turn out to be correct, or saying, "I felt like someone was following me," or "Something about it didn't feel quite right." More often than not, though, we ignore the feeling. This is because we have lost touch with intuition and our ability to trust it.

Decisions, decisions

Trusting in your inner sense is a huge help in making decisions. This is not a fail-safe method; but it means continuing to use your mind, your intellect and your ego as usual, but adding your soul to the decision-making process. The best help will come from a healthy Ajna chakra. Like all the spiritual chakras, it is best balanced through meditation. Someone with an open and balanced third eye chakra is better able to separate truth from illusion, thereby developing trust in their inner wisdom. Using the mindful skills developed in this emotional center allows the person to receive guidance and inspiration from their creativity and intuition. This is emotional intelligence, and it allows the individual to evaluate their conscious and unconscious insights to reach the best decision.

Excessive energy in this chakra can cause difficulties with concentration, headaches, nightmares and even hallucinations. An overactive third eye chakra can also, in some cases, lead to severe emotional disturbances, such as schizophrenia. Deficiencies show themselves as poor memory, eye problems, difficulty recognizing problems, and not being able to visualize well. In the modern world, we often suffer from these problems due to the busy lives we lead. Too much time looking at computer screens, social media and rushing from here to there can affect our ability to focus or switch off. Having time away from these all-encompassing technologies and just sitting with yourself can recharge your third eye chakra and, in turn, help you when you need to concentrate, relax or sleep.

The yantra and associated deities

The lotus flower of the Ajna yantra has only two white petals, which sit on each side of a white circle. These are variously represented as wings, our physical eyes and the topmost point where the Ida and Pingala *nadis* (channels) that carry our *prana* (life force) meet. This reminds us of the duality in all things— the highest point at which our rising vitality and our descending energy meet. The white circle represents the void, which exists beyond the five senses. Inside the circle, a crescent moon represents the Ajna vortex and a red dot shows how the body is able to rise above the sexual energy of the body symbolized by the upside-down triangle below. The triangle also symbolizes wisdom, the yoni (female sexual organ) and the trinity of the godhead. Inside it is the symbol of the mantra, om, and a lingam (male sexual organ). Deities associated with this yantra are Shiva and Hakini Shakti, the aspect of the feminine divine linked to this chakra.

The bija (seed) mantra

Om (pronounced "aum," see page 43-44) is the most renowned and expansive of the bija mantras. It is the mantra of assent and the form of creation, causing energy to surge upward and outward. It is used with the sixth chakra because chanting it is said to be able to open the third eye by physically merging the left and right hemispheres of the brain. According to Paramahansa Yogananda (author of *Autobiography of a Yogi*), "Om or Aum of the *Vedas* became the sacred word *Hum* of the Tibetans, *Amin* of the Muslims and *Amen* of the Egyptians, Greeks, Romans, Jews and Christians." The word has been translated into many different languages, cultures and religious traditions, but the creative and transformative power of the sound remains the same.

Meditations

Meditation is the most effective way of opening the third eye chakra. But people have different reactions to the process. Some experience flashing images of things they are familiar with: nature, waterfalls, people and trains, for example. Others describe it as being able to see your thoughts, almost as if they are scrolling by on a blackboard.

It is common to have a headache during your first attempts to activate the third eye. Don't worry—as you continue to

practice, the headaches will go away. To train yourself to more fully appreciate the third eye, try focusing on one particular image. It could be a number, it could be an object—just try to keep your mind centered on whatever image you have chosen.

If you aren't able to get in touch with the third eye immediately, don't worry. Meditation can take a while to get used to, and activating the third eye even longer.

1   Sit down in comfortable manner for meditation. Slowly blink your eyes closed. Take a few long and deep breaths. As you exhale, bring your attention to the center of your forehead, in between the brows and just above the brow line, and imagine an indigo-blue chakra. Watch as the dark indigo glow of the chakra illuminates your mind and then spreads to the rest of your body.

2   Imagine an entrance to your mind through the third eye. Open the door and walk into an empty room. Imagine the room any way you like—choose the color, decor, look and feel. Make it suit your tastes perfectly, so that it becomes your personal sanctuary.

3 Find the most comfortable spot in the room and sit down. Look out onto the world from there. Bring into focus the same thoughts, issues, situations and ideas that occupy your day-to-day life. Silently contemplate them.

4 Now imagine your sixth chakra spinning and gaining strength. As it spins faster, its indigo light washes over you and pervades every cell, every pore in your body.

5 Breathe deeply and feel the energy bursting from your third eye as rays of dazzling deep-blue light.

6 Rest in this awareness for a few moments, gazing at the world in this new, clean light.

7 When you are finished, gently stand up and walk to the door through which you entered the room. Walk out and look back at your inner sanctuary and feel one with it before closing the door. Then imagine returning to your body. Breathe.

8 When you are ready, blink your eyes open, stand up and go on with your day.

✷ ✷ ✷

1 Sit down in a comfortable position for meditation. Slowly blink your eyes closed. Keep your head up, your chest open and your back straight. Place your hands in your lap or your knees.

2 Breathe in and out. Be mindful of your body and how it feels in the moment. If there are aches in your body, work on relaxing those before you begin. Focus on each part of your body in turn as you sit and relax.

3 When you are ready, focus on the present moment. Feel your body expand and contract with each breath. Be aware of how your breath goes in and out. Try to focus entirely on your breathing. Take a deep breath (inhale for a count of three, then exhale for a count of three); repeat with two more deep breaths.

4 When you are ready, start focusing on your third eye at the center of your forehead. Under your eyelids, move your eyes up toward the third eye. Keep them focused there throughout the meditation. Begin counting backwards from one hundred.

5 By the time you have reached zero, you should be ready to access the third eye. If you are properly focused, everything will be dark except the third eye. Your brain will be relaxed but functioning at a new level. Both sides of the brain will be working together and you will be aware of the energy around you.

6   You can also tell if your third eye has been activated when you are able to focus strongly on just one object and your mind is completely consumed by holding that image. Stay in that moment for a while.

7   When you are ready, bring yourself slowly out of the meditation. Move your eyes away from the third eye. Stay relaxed, but become more aware of your breath. Be mindful of the way your breath goes in and out. Sometimes counting helps to put more focus on your breath as you are coming out of your meditation. Blink your eyes open and return to your day.

The Seventh Chakra
SAHASRARA

COMMON NAME
The crown chakra

LOCATION
The top of the head

ELEMENT
Thought

COLOR
Violet

SENSE
None

BIJA (SEED) MANTRA
Silence/Om

YANTRA SYMBOL
1,000-petaled lotus flower; the petals, of different colors, are arranged in 20 layers

with 50 petals in each layer. Inside is an upward-pointing triangle

ASSOCIATED DEITIES
Shiva, Shakti

GEMS AND STONES
Sapphire, amethyst, celestite

The seventh and last chakra, Sahasrara, is unlike the others in several ways. Most importantly, it sits outside the body and is therefore not directly associated with the physical. Some say it sits on top of the head, others that it is slightly above; both descriptions explain its common name of the crown chakra. Unlike the other chakras, Sahasrara does not affect specific aspects of our lives. If your seventh chakra is unbalanced, you are unlikely to notice any physical symptoms. Unlike the others, healing this chakra does not require a difficult yoga *asana*, or the chanting of a specific mantra (although some associate om with Sahasrara). Instead it requires nothing but silence, meditation and patient waiting…

This is also the hardest chakra to introduce to the beginner. For many, in this task-focused modern digital age, talk of spiritual development, enlightenment and living in a state of pure awareness can be hard to take seriously. It can be difficult to reconcile the pursuit of awareness of a higher consciousness with the demands of our daily lives. Cynicism is the most likely response. But you can think about it in another way. In our own ways, we have all had moments of joy, of extreme happiness, of clarity, of contentment. Can these not be described as "moments of pure awareness"? Practicing meditation, prayer if you want to do it, and daily silence are disciplines that lead to increased moments of spiritual connection and longer moments of pure awareness. The more you practice these, the better you will get.

The brain, the mind and the universe

Because of its location on top of the head, the crown chakra is closely associated with the brain and the endocrine system, notably the pineal and pituitary glands. The endocrine system is the collection of glands that produce hormones regulating growth and development, tissue function, metabolism, sexual function, reproduction, sleep and mood among other things. The brain is the center of the nervous system. Physiologically, it works like a big computer, processing information that it receives from the senses and the body, and sending messages back to the body. It is the most complex organ in the human body and exerts centralized control over all the other organs.

The brain's statistics are astonishing: it contains approximately 86 billion nerve cells (neurons), each one capable of transmitting 1,000 impulses per second, which travel at the same speed as Formula One cars. A piece of brain tissue the size of a grain of sand contains 100,000 neurons and a billion synapses, all communicating with each other. There are 100,000 miles of blood vessels in the brain—the distance around the world at the equator is 24,900 miles! The brain plays a key role in how we pay attention, our perception, awareness, thought, memory and language. But even these facts pale into insignificance when you think that the brain contains your consciousness. Your consciousness is made up of everything you have experienced in your life: your memories, your loves, your likes and dislikes, and the knowledge that one day it will end. It is astonishing to think that, at every moment, you carry everything with you inside your head. Your mind has no limits, no time constraints, no connection to the material world and no locality. Sahasrara represents that freedom—no wonder we should look after it.

Internal quiet

Experiencing Sahasrara is a rare thing. But looking for, and finding, quiet moments of liberation, love, contentment and even bliss less so, and that too is Sahasrara. In today's fractured world, finding moments like these has become more and more important. To find this "bliss," we need to silence the chatter (*vrittis*) in our minds; we need to cultivate an internal quiet. This does not come easily.

The crown chakra is associated with the following psychological and behavioral characteristics:

* Consciousness

* Awareness of higher consciousness, knowledge of what is sacred

* Connection with the formless, the limitless

* Realization

* Liberation from limiting patterns

* Communion with higher states of consciousness: ecstasy and bliss

* Presence

Keeping it in balance is therefore essential for our well-being, spiritual and otherwise. For some, this chakra is the gateway to the cosmic self or the divine self, to universal consciousness. It's linked to the infinite, the universal. For others, it is a state of pure happiness and contentment. For some, Sahasrara has been lost; for others it has always been here. All we need to do is search for it.

A balanced seventh chakra allows us access to the utmost clarity and enlightened wisdom. Its energy is able to generate a blissful union with all that exists. This is regarded as spiritual ecstasy. However, an imbalance in this chakra can manifest itself as a feeling of disconnection to the spirit, a cynical attitude to what is sacred, a disconnection from the body, from earthly matters and an attitude of closed-mindedness.

Help is at hand to restore this chakra to balance through meditation (see page 116) and yoga (see pages 124-141). But a very effective alternative exists in the form of *pranayama* (alternate nostril breathing). This breathing practice balances and activates the Ida and Pingala *nadis* (see page 102):

1   Sit in a comfortable position, either on a chair or on the floor, perhaps in your favorite position for meditation.

2 Place your left hand on your left thigh or knee and move your right hand up toward your face. Rest your index and middle fingers at the third eye.

3 Place your thumb on your right nostril and inhale through the left nostril. Hold your breath for 2–3 seconds. Now close the left nostril with your last two fingers and release and exhale from the right nostril. Again, inhale from the right, close the right nostril with the thumb and then exhale from the left. Repeat the procedure 5–7 times on each side.

The yantra and associated deities

The yantra for the seventh chakra is unlike any of the others. In Sanskrit, the name *sahasrara*, means "thousandfold," and the lotus used here is said to have a thousand petals. The petals, arranged in 20 layers with 50 petals in each, come in all the colors of the rainbow. In some versions, the lotus appears to be bell-shaped, almost hat-like; in others, it is depicted simply as a circle. The lotus has been a potent emblem in India for more than two thousand years. The plant grows in muddy water and bursts into bloom when it rises to the surface, symbolizing human growth and the nurturing of our spiritual selves as we rise toward the sun.

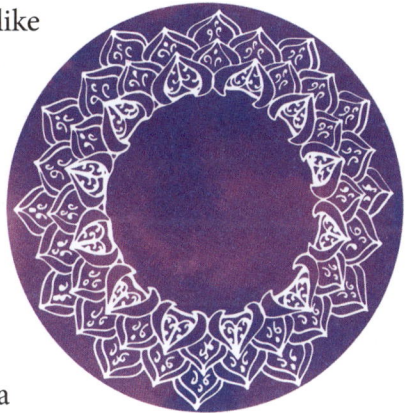

The bija (seed) mantra

For some, the seventh chakra has no mantra, and is best opened through silent meditation. For others, like the sixth chakra, Ajna, the seventh is associated with the mantra *om* (see pages 43-44). This is said to help cultivate a connection with the spirit and the whole universe or higher power. It can also help reduce overattachment to material things and the physical world. Some believe it stimulates the pituitary gland in the brain.

There are four parts to the seed mantra om. They are: "ahh," "ooo" and "mmm" and the silence that follows. "Ahh" represents the start of the universe. As you vibrate with it, you could feel it above your stomach. "Ooo" represents the energy of the universe, and you will feel its vibrations in your chest. "Mmm" represents transformation. As you vibrate the sound, you should feel it in your brain. The last sound, when the long "mmm" has ceased, takes us into the deep silence of the Infinite, the Void itself, that of Infinite Consciousness.

Meditations

1   Sit in a comfortable place for meditation. Take a long and deep breath. As you exhale, move your attention to the top of your head and imagine a violet chakra. The dark violet glow of the chakra illuminates your mind and your body.

2 Imagine a big, white lotus with its petals closed in the same place as your crown chakra. Look at the lotus and contemplate its shape, color and texture.

3 As you pay attention, the lotus slowly starts to swirl along with the chakra.

4 One by one, the petals of the lotus start to open. As the first layer flowers, you see uncountable rows of more petals still to open.

5 With every new petal opening the lotus starts spinning faster. You realize that every such opening leads to yet another layer of closed petals. The blooming of the lotus is a process of infinite stages.

6 Now see your seventh chakra spinning with equal strength. The chakra's violet light washes over you and fills every cell, every pore of your body.

7 Breathe deeply and feel the energy from your crown chakra connecting you to the sky above and to the earth below, and to everything in between, so you become one with existence.

8 Rest in this awareness.

9 When you are ready, blink your eyes open and stand up, ready for the rest of your day.

* * *

1 If you can, find a quiet place outside: in your yard, on the roof, or somewhere private. In the evening or the night would be preferable. Take a candle or a flashlight of some kind to help you find your way. If you can't, then indoors is fine too.

2 Sit down in a comfortable position for meditation. Place your right hand over your heart, and let the fingertips of your left hand graze the ground beside you. Close your eyes. Settle into your seat, feeling the solidity of the ground beneath you, the support of your connection to the earth. Out of that support, allow your spine to rise and the crown of your head to soar into the heavens.

3 Connect to the flow of your breath. Feel the sacred quality of that connection—this process of inhale and exhale that is with you for the duration of this body's time here.

4 Sensing each rise and fall—each coming and going—in its fullness, ask yourself, Where does this breath come from?

5 Is it possible for you to consider that, as you breathe in and out, a force beyond you is providing the very breath to you that sustains your life? It is within you and all around you. It is the stuff of everything, and beyond this body and this life. Can you be open to such a possibility?

6   If you can, allow yourself to name this force in your life: Spirit, Mother, God, Love... Contemplate this presence... What might it look like to you, feel like to you? When do you feel most connected to the sacred?

7   When you are ready, bring your attention back to your breath. Exist in your breathing. Then, gently blink your eyes open, move your fingers, arms and legs, and stand up. After a moment or two, you can get up and continue with your evening.

Part Three

CARING FOR YOUR CHAKRAS

Moving into balance

Caring for yourself, for your body, for your spirit, for your mental and physical health, starts with awareness—awareness of your lifestyle, the things you eat and drink, how much you exercise, your ethics and morals, and so on. It is important that we choose how we want to live our lives. Of course, no one chooses to suffer ill health, but life does inflict wear and tear on both body and mind, whatever lifestyle we choose.

As we have seen, chakras have been a part of people's lives for over 2,000 years and, if you have read this far, you have now joined that group. By now you will have developed an awareness of the seven major chakras, and by meditating on them, as described in the chapters on the individual chakras, you will have been able to open them up and begin to develop an awareness of how they feel, how they might affect you, and whether they are balanced. In this section, we are going to look more closely at how to develop a regular care regimen for them, and how to heal or realign them if they become unbalanced or blocked.

We have already examined the benefits of meditation in your regular chakra care, and it is a good idea to start any session on chakras with a few moments of meditation, perhaps combined with some appropriate mantra chants. In terms of healing, yoga poses, which are often known by the Sanskrit word *asanas*, are by far the most effective method. The chakras have been linked with the practice of yoga since the 10th century BCE, a connection that is still holding strong. This is thought to be because the practice of bending, stretching and twisting *asanas* helps our energy and life-force (*prana*) flow through our bodies.

If practiced regularly, yoga is likely to keep your chakras well balanced. For this purpose, they are best done in order (starting at the bottom and moving up the spine), one after the other. However, if you develop a blockage, the healing *asanas* that follow have been chosen with each specific chakra in mind to help you target any one for particular attention.

Note

Yoga should be taken seriously. Done incorrectly or inappropriately, it can result in injury. The best way to practice it is to join a reputable school, or join a class run by an accredited yoga teacher. If you are pregnant, recovering from an operation, suffer from back pain, high blood pressure, heart problems, unsteady blood pressure or sugar levels, or are recovering from a hip, knee or back fracture, you should not be attempting to practice these poses.

If you feel any pain when practicing yoga, please stop immediately. Never push your body beyond its natural limits in any pose. If in doubt, please see a doctor for advice.

Balance the chakras with yoga

You need to do a little preparation for a yoga session. Much of this will be the same as for a meditation session, but it is helpful to remind yourself of these things before you start, so you're not interrupted or disturbed. Find a quiet and preferably uncluttered room in your home for yoga practice. Dress in comfortable clothes that allow you to move easily. Loose-fitting sweatpants or leggings and a T-shirt are ideal. Yoga is always practiced in bare feet. It is essential that you have a yoga mat.

You may have demands on your time that dictate when you can do yoga, but with the rays of the early-morning sun coming through the window would be ideal. Open the window to let in some fresh air, if appropriate. Plan to do your session before a meal rather than afterward, and make sure you listen to the call of nature before you start. Drink a little water if you are thirsty. You are now ready to warm up.

Start with a simple breathing practice. The exercise below is designed to encourage even, steady breaths.

BREATH AWARENESS

1 Sit on a chair, placing your feet on the ground, hip-width apart, with your knees directly above. If your feet don't reach the floor, use books or blocks to support them. Alternatively, sit on the floor

cross-legged if you are comfortable doing so, using a firm pillow or cushion to sit on so that your back does not collapse. You can also place supports under your knees if they are uncomfortable.

2 For either seated position, gently press the sitting bones down and lengthen the spine so it is upright but not rigid. Relax the shoulders down, away from the ears. Rest your hands on your lap. Gently close your eyes if you are comfortable doing so; otherwise half-close them and cast your gaze softly downwards.

3 Mentally scan your body from the head downwards, noticing any areas where you are holding tension—the facial muscles, the shoulders, the abdominal area. And notice areas that feel open and relaxed, not tense. Notice all the different sensations of the body.

4 Now bring your awareness to your breath. Without trying to change it, start to observe the quality of the breath—the texture, the rhythm, the speed. Is the in breath shorter or longer than the out breath? Notice all the varying sensations of the breath as it flows in and out of your body.

5 Watch each breath for its duration, observing with acceptance (rather than frustration if it doesn't meet your expectations).

6 After a few minutes, start to follow your out breath from its start to its end. Notice whether you allow it to run all the way to the end,

or whether you curtail it and start breathing in before you have fully breathed out. If this is the case, see if you can allow the out breath to reach its natural conclusion.

7 Be patient, and don't worry if it's not possible. It is a process. The most important thing is for the breath to be natural and not forced.

8 Notice how the navel moves toward the spine toward the end of the out breath, and how there's a natural pause at the end of the out breath if you allow it to take place.

9 Notice how the next in breath arises out of this pause, and how the inhalation will deepen naturally as a result of the fuller out breath.

10 Follow the breath for a few minutes, and when you are ready to end the practice, slowly bring your awareness back and start to gently move the arms, legs, fingers and toes before standing up.

After the breathing exercise, give yourself a few moments to gather your thoughts. When you are ready, the following *asana* will help you engage the chakras in preparation for the particular healing pose or poses you want to practice. If you're a complete beginner, or unsteady on your feet, then you can try it sitting in a chair. Use a chair that offers firm support. If you are going to use a chair, you must ensure that your feet are firmly on the ground, hip-width apart, and your knees are in line with your ankles.

TADASANA (MOUNTAIN POSE)

1 Stand with your feet hip-width apart. Ensure your feet are in line with each other.

2 Root down with the heels and the balls of your feet, spread and extend your toes, draw up the foot arches.

3 Draw your knees and thigh muscles upwards.

4 Press the top of the inner thighs back and the tailbone forward. Draw the lower abdomen and navel in and up.

5 Lengthen the spine upwards, lift the breastbone, allowing the shoulders to relax back and down; broaden the chest.

6 Lift the crown of the head up while pressing the soles of the feet down, particularly the heels and the mounds of the toes, into the ground.

7 Extend your arms down the sides of the body, palms facing your thighs. Gaze straight ahead and breathe steadily. Remain in the pose for 20 seconds.

Root chakra healing pose

Vrksasana (Tree pose)

1 Stand in Tadasana (see page 127).

2 Put your weight on your left foot; raise your right leg and bend it at the knee. Place your raised foot on the inner thigh or the inner shin of your left leg. (Avoid placing the foot on the inner knee.) Your toes should be pointing downwards.

3 Join your palms together at the heart (as in prayer position).

4 If you feel unstable, place a hand on the wall for support.

5 Let your spine lengthen upward as you press the foot of your standing leg firmly down.

6 Feel the sense of being grounded as you root down.

7 Gaze straight ahead at eye level. This will help you balance.

8 Stay as long as feels comfortable, and then return to Tadasana.

9 Repeat on the other side.

'Like a tree you have to find your roots, and then you can bend in the wind'
Angela Farmer

Sacral chakra healing pose

Utkata Konasana (Goddess pose)

1   Stand in Tadasana (see page 127).

2   Step your feet wide apart (about 3-4 feet, depending on your height). Turn your toes slightly out.

3   Start to bend your knees, extending them in the same direction as your toes. Make sure your knees are correctly aligned and not collapsing inward.

4   Lower your hips down to the height of your knees, if possible, but only go as far as feels comfortable. Take the tailbone slightly forwards and lengthen the spine upwards, keeping the torso as upright as possible.

5   Press down evenly on the soles of the feet.

6   Extend your arms out to the sides at shoulder height. Bend your arms at the elbows, so your palms face forward and the fingers upward, to form a right angle.

7   If you have a shoulder injury, rest your hands on your thighs.

8   Stay in the pose for 20-30 seconds, or as long as feels comfortable, then press through the feet to come up. Then bring the feet back together.

Navel chakra healing pose

Virabhadrasana (Warrior I pose)

1 Stand in Tadasana (see page 127).

2 Turn to the side of your mat, and extend your feet approximately 3-4 feet apart.

3 Raise your arms above your head with palms facing each other. Yours arms should be straight and shoulder-width apart. (If your shoulders are tight or uncomfortable, take your arms wider apart.)

4 Turn your right foot 90 degrees to the right, and turn your back foot in to the right.

5 Bend your right knee. Your right knee should be positioned over your right heel, not collapsing inward and not going beyond the heel.

6 Press down on your left outer heel; press your inner left thigh back; take your tailbone forward. Stretch your body upward. Gaze straight ahead.

7 Hold for 15-20 seconds, then come up out of the pose. Repeat on other side.

Heart chakra healing pose

Bhujangasana (Cobra pose)

1 Lie prone (front-side down) on the floor.

2 Stretch your legs back and press the front of your thighs and feet into the ground. Draw your tailbone to the ground.

3 Place your hands flat on the floor by the sides of your chest with your elbows hugging the sides of your body.

4 On an inhalation, start to lift your chest off the ground by pressing your hands firmly down and starting to straighten the arms.

5 Draw the navel up toward the chest, drop the shoulders down away from the ears, and lift the sternum without the front ribs flaring.

6 Ensure the backbend is evenly distributed throughout the spine to avoid putting pressure on the lower back.

7 Do not strain the back by trying to come up too high. Keeping the elbows bent rather than straightening the arms completely will help avoid potential strain.

8 Stay in the pose for up to 30 seconds, then, on an exhalation, lower your body down and rest.

Throat chakra healing pose

Setu Bandha Sarvangasana (Bridge pose)

1 Lie supine (on your back) on the ground, then bend your knees and place your feet firmly on the ground with your heels directly under your knees; your feet should be parallel and hip-width apart.

2 Extend your arms by the sides of your body, with palms face-down. Press the arms into the ground.

3 Press down with your feet to lift your hips slowly off the ground, using your arms for support. Extend your tailbone toward the knees to lengthen your lower back; then lift a little more (never forcing) and move your chest in the direction of your chin.

4 Check that your thighs remain parallel, lifting your outer hips up and releasing your inner thighs down toward the floor.

5 Remain in this position for approximately 30 seconds, or as long as feels comfortable, and then slowly come down.

Third eye chakra healing pose

Balasana
(Child's pose)

1 Kneel down on all fours.

2 Your knees should be slightly more than hip-width apart. Bring your big toes together. Move your sitting bones back to rest on your heels. You can place a rolled-up blanket or towel under your feet if there is discomfort in the front of the feet, and/or, similarly, between the backs of your thighs and your calves if your sitting bones don't reach your heels.

3 On an exhalation, bend forward from the hips, keeping the front of your body long, and rest your torso between your thighs.

4 Place your forehead on the ground, or, if it does not reach the ground, rest your forehead on a block (or book). Your head should not hang without support. Observe the place where your forehead meets the ground or support.

5 Extend your arms out in front of you, palms face-down.

6 This is a resting pose—there should be no discomfort in your knees, legs, shoulders or back. Let your breath be easy and fluid.

7 Rest in this position for up to 2 minutes.

8 Exit the pose on an inhalation, pressing your hands into the floor to lift your body.

Crown chakra healing pose

Savasana
(Corpse pose)

This is an excellent exercise to rebalance the crown chakra, but it can also be used to finish any chakra healing session.

1 Sit on the floor, extend your legs out in front of you and slowly lower yourself to the ground until you are lying supine.

2 Let your arms and legs fall away from the sides of your body. Turn your palms to face the ceiling, let your legs and feet relax out to the sides. Ensure your limbs are as symmetrical as possible to enable optimal relaxation.

3 Place a pillow under your knees if there is any tension in your back; alternatively, you can support the lower legs on the seat of a chair.

4 Place a folded blanket under your head and neck if your head is tilted backwards.

5 Close your eyes and allow your body to relax; surrender the weight of the body to the ground beneath you.

6 Keep your attention on your breathing, and try to remain completely still.

7 Stay in the pose for up to 5 minutes, then slowly bring your awareness back, open your eyes, draw your knees up and over to the right and then push yourself up to a seated position.

Feeding the Chakras

Keeping your energy points in balance is helped by a healthy diet. The best diets are based around a little meat—if you are a carnivore—plus vegetables, grains and fruits. We are all encouraged to "eat the rainbow," and this is a philosophy based on Ayurveda, the "science of life," a system used in India for thousands of years to bring the body into a healthy and vitalized state of balance. Food of certain colors encourages healing in your body. Choosing foods of colors that are in tune with the

colors of the chakras, the cycle of the seasons, and the time of the day will help develop a calm and nourished body. Spend a bit of time choosing the freshest possible meat, vegetables and fruit.

MULADHARA

The root chakra is represented by the color red, for energy. If you are feeling run down, fatigued, burnt out, lazy or lethargic, red foods such as tomatoes, strawberries, raspberries, radishes, pumpkins and beets will help boost your energy levels and your body temperature. Also choose root vegetables, such as carrots, potatoes and parsnips, as well as onions and garlic. Protein-rich foods like eggs, meat, beans, tofu, soy products and peanut butter will also bring benefits. Cook with spices like paprika and pepper.

SVADHISTHANA

The sacral chakra, also known as the creativity chakra, is located at the navel and associated with the color orange. It governs your confidence and self-worth, so if you are low on these and feel unworthy of love then eat sweet fruits like mangoes, melons and oranges. Vegetables such as carrots, sweet potatoes and butternut squash will also help you regain control and balance in your life. Honey and nuts are also recommended. For cooking, use spices like cinnamon and vanilla to add flavor.

MANIPURA

This is called the solar plexus chakra, affects your ego and self-esteem, and is represented by the color yellow. Yellow food is a natural mood enhancer, so if you are sad or depressed, eat fruit like pineapple or bananas, or vegetables such as corn on the cob or yellow peppers. Dairy products like milk, cheese and yogurt are also helpful, as are grains such as rice, cereals, flax and sunflower seeds. Robust spices, such as ginger, mint, turmeric and cumin will flavor your cooking, along with more subtle flavors from chamomile and fennel.

ANAHATA

The heart chakra, associated with matters of love, of course, is also affected by stress, fatigue and acidity. Its color is green, and the healing process can be helped by eating leafy vegetables such as spinach, broccoli, cauliflower, cabbage and kale. You could even put them in the juicer for a healthy breakfast drink. Either that or serve up a big salad with the tastiest leaves you can find, adding some avocado and grapes along with basil, thyme and cilantro. Green tea during the day can also help in rejuvenating a steady emotional frame of mind.

VISHUDDHA

This chakra is associated with the throat, and represents our power and responsibility through the way we communicate. If this chakra is blocked, we might have difficulty in expressing ourselves, perhaps because of a cold, a sore throat or an ear infection. It is associated with the colors blue and black, and a healthy bowl of blueberries or blackberries is sure to hit the spot. Tree fruits, such as apples, pears, peaches and plums, are also helpful. To soothe a sore throat, drink water, fruit juice and herbal tea.

AJNA

The third eye, as it is popularly known, is located in the center of the brow of your head, just above the eyebrows. It is the seat of wisdom, intuition and perspective and can therefore be vulnerable to frustration and anger when out of balance. Feed it with foods that are calming such as chocolate, maybe washed down with a little red wine. This chakra's color is indigo, so try cooking purple food such as eggplant, make a salad with radicchio, or go for a simple plate of fresh grapes, plums and figs. You can also boost the flavors of your cooking with allspice, cardamom or sage.

SAHASRARA

The highest form of chakra, called the crown chakra, represents your higher self and opens up your communication with the universe. In general, this chakra does not need feeding; it benefits from fasting or detoxifying, which can help in awakening spiritual communication. In addition, burning incense such as copal, frankincense and juniper can help cleanse the air around you and nourish the chakra as you meditate.

Healing the Chakras

Yoga, meditation and a selective diet are not the only options open to those wanting to maintain the health and balance of their energy centers. The use of essential oils, energy healing techniques, gems and crystals are also widespread, particularly when it comes to healing. This might involve clearing unwanted energy, like stress, from the system; dissolving blockages, such as pain or tension; increasing the flow of vitality through the body; or even increasing one particular type of positive energy when you need it, like calm or optimism. But do they really work?

Essential oils

Essential oils are aromatic compounds found in the leaves, flowers, roots, stems, bark and seeds of plants. They have been in use since the age of Ancient Egypt for therapeutic, cosmetic and ceremonial purposes, offering the promise of improvement of both mood and health. In plants, the oils serve various functions: assisting pollination, repelling pests and predators, fighting disease and encouraging cell regeneration. For humans, their use is effective in the short and long term as an aid to physical wellness, supporting massage, yoga and meditation, clearing chakras of unwanted energy, and maintaining emotional balance, among other things.

There is scientific proof of this. Essential oils are antibacterial, antiviral, antifungal, antioxidant, sedative, analgesic, antispasmodic, cleansing and antimicrobial. Because of their tiny molecular size, and because they are fat-soluble, essential oils can penetrate cell membranes and therefore pass from the blood into the brain fluid in the central nervous system. Oils can disrupt viruses and repair damaged cell replication. They can clean receptor sites, leading to improved cell communication, reprogram DNA, and deliver oxygen to tissues. They are also used to treat bacteria, such as MRSA, blood clots, stress and disease-causing free radicals. They are known to calm moods, help with relaxation, and improve sleep. It is estimated that 25 percent of commercially available medicines contain plant derivatives. They are used in a number of commercially available products, such as personal-care items, household cleaners, aromatherapy candles and mosquito repellents.

Essential oils enter the body through the nose, skin and mouth, from where they will reach the bloodstream. These multiple methods make oils easy to use for adults and children. Perhaps the most common use is through the nose. Many people use a diffuser to scent a room, creating a range of atmospheres, though they are also useful to inhibit airborne bacteria and help those with breathing difficulties. For an instant hit, you can simply put a drop of oil in the palm of your hand, rub both hands together, and breathe it in. Because oils can be calming, soothing and energizing, and because they have easy access to the brain, this is a fast and easy way to affect mood. Essential oils are often used in clinics and hospitals because of their calming properties.

Because of their molecular makeup, these oils penetrate the skin quickly, having an instant, localized effect. This kind of application is good for occasional pain, muscle aches, headaches, acne, bruises, burns, rashes and as an insect repellent.

Essential oils can be very strong, and are often diluted with a "carrier" or "base" oil such as coconut or almond oil. It is important to read the label on any essential-oil product to understand the recommended dilution for your purpose. It is particularly important to do this if you have sensitive skin or are using the oils on children or infants (see note below). They are also a wonderful aid for massage, particularly chakra massage. It is believed that our thoughts and actions are absorbed through each chakra. When negative energy flows through a chakra it begins to spin too fast or too slow, making it unbalanced. This can affect us physically, emotionally and spiritually. Massage, reflection, meditation and energy work using essential oils can help restore balance to each of the chakras. There are a number of essential oils that resonate with each chakra. Here is a recommended starter list:

Muladhara (the root chakra)
CEDAR
MYRRH
PATCHOULI

Svadhisthana
(the sacral chakra)
JASMINE
ROSE
YLANG YLANG

Manipura
(the solar plexus chakra)
BLACK PEPPER
CARDAMOM
SAGE

Anahata (the heart chakra)
NEROLI
PINE
ROSEWOOD

Vishuddha (the throat chakra)
CHAMOMILE
FRANKINCENSE
LAVENDER

Ajna (the third eye chakra)
SANDALWOOD
LEMON
ROSEMARY

Sahasrara (the crown chakra)
LIME
MANDARIN ORANGE
FRANKINCENSE

Though it is much rarer, some oils can be ingested. For example, peppermint oil has been found to be effective in combating the effects of Irritable Bowel Syndrome (IBS). However, a number of essential oils are not only extremely strong, they are also toxic. It is also true to say that, like medicines, they can affect people in different ways. So, the advice is **do not ingest essential oils** unless you do so under the advice and guidance of a trained herbalist.

Essential oils have their critics, of course. They can be expensive because of the labor-intensive work involved in producing them. They are also wasteful; for example, it takes 13.5 kilos of lavender flowers to make a 15ml bottle of essential oil. They have potential side effects, which could be serious for babies and pets, and they are unregulated. Please consider the following warning before you consider using them:

Important to note

Essential oils are very strong. If you are pregnant, or are intending to use them on children under 12, it is recommended that you visit your doctor to ask for advice.

If you have sensitive skin and are using an oil for the first time, you should do a skin-sensitivity test first. Put a few drops of diluted oil on your inner thigh and wait 24 hours to see if any irritation or redness occurs.

Avoid application on sensitive areas, like the eyes, genitals, inner ears or broken skin. The best places for application are the soles of the feet, the wrists and the back of the neck. Massage after application increases the blood flow and maximizes absorption.

Energy healing

Energy healing is any therapy that uses the energy of the human body to bring the body back into balance so it can begin to heal itself. Given that these techniques use the body's life-force (*prana* in Hindu practices, *qi* in Chinese medicine), they are closely associated with the chakra energy centers. There are different schools of thought in this area, but those most relevant to the study

of the chakras are reiki, reflexology, acupuncture, color and sound therapy.

Reiki is a Japanese practice that was developed by Dr Mikao Usui in the early 20th century. A Reiki healer uses the palm of their hands, without touching the patient, and uses their own body as a channel to direct universal energy into the patient. During a session, the healer's hands are placed in the auric field (see page 24) over the location of all seven major chakras, usually starting with the crown chakra. Healers are taught not to direct the energy, just to let it flow where it is needed. Reflexology works on the basis that there are pressure points in the feet and the palms of the hands that relate to different parts of the body, and that working with these pressure points can help ease problems in those areas. For maintaining chakra balance, the most important of these is an area along the arch of the foot that controls our spinal reflexes. Thirty seconds of massage on each foot should restore the balance.

Acupuncture originated in China and has become a popular form of alternative healing around the world. The practice involves fine needles being inserted into the skin at various defined points around the body in order to balance the flow of *qi*. Western doctors tend to view the practice as a way to increase blood flow by stimulating the nerves, muscles and connective tissue in various parts of the body rather than proper medicine. But research has shown that acupuncture is helpful in

the treatment of headaches, hypertension, depression, back pain, nausea, rheumatoid arthritis and other conditions.

Color is simply light of varying wavelengths and frequencies. Electromagnetic waves constantly surround us, and color is part of those waves. Every single cell in the body needs light energy. Our cells absorb color, and this affects us on every level: physically, emotionally and spiritually. It is thought that the colors of the rainbow—red, orange, yellow, green, blue, indigo and violet—resonate with the chakras, the body's main energy centers. Color therapy is the practice of visualizing the relevant color, along with repeated exposure to that color, wearing clothes of that color and eating foods of that color (see page 142) in order to speed up the healing processes.

Sound healing, also known as vibrational healing, is believed to date back to Ancient Greece. The basic principle behind it is that the entire universe is in a state of vibration. This includes every organ, cell, bone, tissue and liquid of the human body, and the electromagnetic fields that surround it. If we are not resonating with some part of ourselves or our surroundings, we become dissonant and therefore unhealthy; our naturally healthy frequency becomes a frequency that vibrates without harmony, creating illness. Sound healing might involve listening to music or other sounds, singing, dancing, meditation or playing an instrument in order to restore the harmonic vibrations we need to restore our physical and emotional well-being.

Good vibrations

The ancient Egyptians believed that gemstones had the power to restore health, and they often buried deceased family members with stones tucked into the layers of linen in which their bodies were wrapped. Since then they have gone in and out of fashion, not as a healing aid for ailments, but as a method of soothing the soul. Today they are undergoing something of a resurgence in popularity. Some believe that this is because, in our fast-paced world, more people are turning to old traditions to relieve the stresses of everyday life. Others see gemstones and crystals as a natural antidote to the energy-suck of technology that we deal with at work and at home. However, there are also those who claim we have a sympathetic resonance with crystals, and researchers are said to have been able to detect electrical energy emanating from quartz crystals when they are placed close to a chakra. The stones must be cleansed in water, then placed outdoors in the sunlight or moonlight, which will energize them.

The basic idea is that crystals carry certain energies that can have a positive effect on our own. In a similar way to magnets, crystals and gemstones

use energy to attract or repel. When you place certain stones over certain parts of your body, they interact with your individual chakras. Your energy transforms, vibrates, pulses, moves and shifts in accordance with the properties and energetic signature of the particular crystal.

As you will have read in the chapters on individual chakras, each is associated with a number of gems and stones. These are listed as follows:

Muladhara (the root chakra)
RUBY
BLOODSTONE
GARNET

Anahata (the heart chakra)
JADE
PERIDOT
ROSE QUARTZ

Svadhisthana
(the sacral chakra)
CARNELIAN
FIRE OPAL
TOPAZ

Vishuddha (the throat chakra)
BLUE TOPAZ
AQUAMARINE
LAPIS LAZULI

Ajna (the third eye chakra)
DIAMOND
EMERALD
SAPPHIRE

Manipura
(the solar plexus chakra)
TOPAZ
YELLOW TOURMALINE
EMERALD

Sahasrara (the crown chakra)
SAPPHIRE
AMETHYST
CELESTITE

If you were to visit a "healing crystal" practitioner, they would most likely get you to lie down and relax before placing appropriate stones near the chakra points. This is said to realign, rebalance and reenergize the chakras back to their appropriate functions. Some suggest placing crystals in your home or holding them in your hands while meditating or, indeed, carrying them with you throughout the day.

For some, crystals have been successful in preventing headaches, relieving stress, improving mood, even bringing peace and happiness. But scientists have been unable to prove claims that they work as medicine. If you believe in them, they might make you feel better through the perception of "good vibrations," and that perception may help alleviate some emotional or spiritual stress.

Index

Acknowledgements

Firstly, I would like to thank Vanessa Daubney and Tania O'Donnell at Arcturus Publishing for commissioning the book and seeing it through to publication. Thanks to Dani Leigh for the beautiful design. Special thanks, too, must go to Charlie Hartley, a yoga teacher from Kent certified with the British Wheel of Yoga, whose help, advice, suggestions and detailed instructions on how to achieve the best healing poses were generously given and immensely helpful (www.yogahartley.co.uk). I am also indebted to the following:

Books: the classic work on chakras in the modern age, *Wheels of Life* by Anodea Judith (Llewellyn Publications, Woodbury, Minnesota, 1987/2016), is the best place to start. Also useful in more practical ways was *The Chakra Bible* by Patricia Mercier (Stirling, New York, 2007).

Websites: Wikipedia, in particular the citations which invariably provide you with a comprehensive bibliography on the subject at hand, is always a great place to begin your research. The following websites were also either useful or inspirational, or both, providing ideas and explanations: bodywindow.com, brettlarkin.com, britannica.com, chopra.com, gaia. com, hareesh.org, mindbodygreen.com, newworldencyclopedia.org, spiritualresearchfoundation.org, timesofindia.com, wanderlust.com, yogapedia.com

Picture Credits